© 2024 by FAISAL JAMIL. All rights reserved.

Title: "Ace Your Interview: 100 Powerful Questions and Top-Scoring Answers for Your Job Interview Success"

This book, along with its contents encompassing text, illustrations, images, diagrams, and other creative elements, is the exclusive property of FAISAL JAMIL and is safeguarded by copyright law.

FAISAL JAMIL asserts full ownership and retains all rights to this book. No part of this publication may be reproduced, distributed, or transmitted in any form or by any means, such as photocopying, recording, or electronic methods, without prior written consent from the copyright holder. Brief quotations in critical reviews and certain noncommercial uses permitted by copyright law are exceptions.

This copyright notice applies to all editions, formats, and translations of the book, whether in print, digital, or any other medium or technology existing now or developed in the future. Unauthorized use or infringement may result in legal action and pursuit of remedies under applicable copyright laws.

While efforts have been made to ensure accuracy and reliability, FAISAL JAMIL does not guarantee the completeness or suitability of the information. Readers are responsible for evaluating and using the content judiciously.

FAISAL JAMIL reserves the right to make changes, updates, or corrections to the book without prior notice. Inclusion of third-party materials or references does not imply endorsement or affiliation unless used under fair use principles or with proper permissions and attributions.

For permissions, inquiries, or requests regarding the book's use, please contact FAISAL JAMIL through official channels listed on their Amazon author page or provided email address.

This comprehensive copyright notice serves to protect FAISAL JAMIL'S intellectual property rights, maintain content control, and inform users about associated restrictions and permissions.

Warm regards,

FAISAL JAMIL

For your feedback and reviews:

http://www.amazon.com/author/faisal.jamil

Email: faisaljamilauthor@gmail.com

About the author

Certainly! Faisal Jamil is a multifaceted individual with a diverse set of skills and experiences. With a strong foundation in computer knowledge since childhood, he has developed a deep understanding of technology that informs his work as a content writer. Faisal also possesses digital skills, which further enhance his abilities in various digital platforms and technologies.

Beyond his professional endeavors, Faisal Jamil has also excelled in the martial arts, particularly Shotokan Karate, where he achieved the prestigious rank of first Dan black belt. This achievement speaks to his dedication, discipline, and commitment to personal growth and mastery.

In his professional life, Faisal Jamil has carved out a successful career in sales management within the Fast Moving Consumer Goods (FMCG) sector. His roles in various FMCG companies have honed his skills in strategic planning, team leadership, and business development. Faisal's ability to drive sales and achieve targets has been instrumental in his career progression, showcasing his talent for identifying opportunities and delivering results.

Faisal Jamil is also deeply interested in business investment strategies, planning, and execution. His understanding of these areas has been key to his success in the business world, allowing him to make informed decisions and implement effective strategies. His ability to navigate the complexities of investment planning and execution has set him apart as a strategic thinker and a valuable asset in any business endeavor.

Overall, Faisal Jamil is a dynamic individual who combines his passion for technology, martial arts, sales management, digital skills, and business investment strategies to achieve success in diverse fields. His journey is a testament to his versatility, resilience, and continuous pursuit of excellence.

Yours Sincerely

FAISAL JAMIL

For your feedback and reviews:

https://www.amazon.com/author/faisal.jamil

Email: faisaljamilauthor@gmail.com

ACE YOUR INTERVIEW 100 POWERFUL QUESTIONS AND TOP-SCORING ANSWERS FOR YOUR JOB INTERIEW SUCCESS

Introduction

Congratulations on taking the first step towards landing your dream job! Job interviews can be nerve-wracking, but with the right preparation, you can confidently answer even the most difficult questions. This book is designed to help you do just that. Inside, you'll find 100 of the most common and challenging interview questions, along with top-scoring answers that will impress any interviewer. Whether you're a seasoned professional or just starting out, this book will equip you with the tools you need to succeed.

Whether you're preparing for your first job interview or your hundredth, this book will help you approach each interview with confidence and professionalism. With practice, preparation, and the right mindset, you can ace any interview and land the job of your dreams.

Table of Content

Preface

Chapter 1: Before the Interview

Chapter 2: During the Interview

Chapter 3: After the Interview

Chapter 4: 100 Interview Questions and Answers

Chapter 5: Conclusion

Preface

Welcome to "Ace Your Interview: 100 Powerful Questions and Top-Scoring Answers for Your Job Interview Success." This book is designed to be your comprehensive guide to mastering the interview process and landing the job of your dreams. Whether you're a seasoned professional looking to advance your career or a recent graduate preparing for your first job interview, this book has something for everyone.

In today's competitive job market, it's more important than ever to stand out from the crowd. Employers are looking for candidates who not only have the right skills and experience but also demonstrate strong communication skills, problem-solving abilities, and a positive attitude. This book will help you develop and showcase these qualities, giving you the edge you need to succeed.

The book is divided into several chapters, each focusing on a different aspect of the interview process. We'll start by helping you understand the job description and research the company, so you can tailor your answers to the specific requirements of the position. We'll then move on to strategies for answering common interview questions, handling difficult questions, and showcasing your skills and experience.

One of the key features of this book is the "100 Interview Questions and Answers" section. Here, you'll find a comprehensive list of common interview questions, along with top-scoring answers for each question. These answers are designed to help you showcase your qualifications, experience, and personality in the best possible light.

Throughout the book, you'll also find practical tips, expert advice, and real-life examples to help you prepare for your interview with confidence. By following the advice in this book, you'll be well on your way to acing your interview and landing the job of your dreams.

So, whether you're just starting your job search or looking to take the next step in your career, "Ace Your Interview" is here to help. Good luck, and happy interviewing!

Chapter 1

Before the Interview

A: Understanding the Job Description

Understanding the job description is a crucial first step in preparing for a job interview. It allows you to tailor your answers to match the specific requirements of the position and demonstrate how your skills and experience make you a perfect fit. Here's how you can effectively understand the job description:

1: Read Carefully:

Start by carefully reading the job description multiple times. Highlight key responsibilities, qualifications, and any specific skills or experiences required for the role.

2: Identify Keywords:

Pay attention to keywords or phrases used in the job description, such as "team player," "detail-oriented," or "strong communication skills." These are often qualities that the employer values and will likely ask about in the interview.

3: Match Your Skills:

Compare the job requirements to your own skills and experiences. Identify areas where your skills align with what the employer is looking for, and be prepared to discuss how you can contribute to the role.

4: Research the Company:

Use the job description to learn more about the company's values, goals, and culture. This will help you tailor your answers to show how you align with the company's values and how you can contribute to its success.

5: Prepare Relevant Examples:

Based on the job description, think of specific examples from your past experiences that demonstrate your ability to meet the job requirements. Be ready to share these examples during the interview to illustrate your qualifications.

6: Ask Clarifying Questions:

If there are any parts of the job description that are unclear, don't hesitate to ask for clarification during the interview. This shows your attention to detail and your interest in the role.

By understanding the job description thoroughly, you can effectively showcase your qualifications and suitability for the position during the interview, increasing your chances of success.

B: Researching the Company

Researching the company is a crucial step in preparing for a job interview. It allows you to understand the company's culture, values, goals, and current projects, which can help you tailor your answers and demonstrate your interest in the role. Here's how you can effectively research a company:

1: Company Website:

Start by visiting the company's official website. Look for information about the company's history, mission, values, products or services, and key personnel. Pay attention to any recent news or press releases, as well as any awards or recognition the company has received.

2: Social Media:

Check the company's social media profiles, such as LinkedIn, Facebook, Twitter, and Instagram. This can give you insights into the company's culture, recent activities, and how it engages with its audience.

3: News and Media:

Search for news articles, press releases, and industry reports related to the company. This can help you understand the company's position in the market, recent developments, and any challenges or opportunities it may be facing.

4: Company Reviews:

Look for reviews from current and former employees on websites like Glassdoor or Indeed. This can give you an idea of the company's culture, work environment, and how employees feel about working there.

5: Networking:

Reach out to current or former employees of the company through professional networking sites like LinkedIn. Ask them about their experiences working at the company and any advice they have for someone interviewing there.

6: Industry Insights:

Research the company's industry and competitors to understand the broader context in which the company operates. This can help you demonstrate your knowledge of the industry during the interview.

7: Prepare Questions:

Based on your research, prepare thoughtful questions to ask during the interview. This shows your genuine interest in the company and your proactive approach to learning more about the role and the organization.

By thoroughly researching the company, you can demonstrate your interest and enthusiasm for the role during the interview, which can set you apart from other candidates and increase your chances of success.

C: Anticipating Questions Based on the Job Requirements

Anticipating questions based on the job requirements is an essential part of interview preparation. By understanding the key responsibilities and qualifications outlined in the job description, you can anticipate the types of questions the interviewer is likely to ask and prepare thoughtful, relevant answers. Here's how you can effectively anticipate questions:

1: Review the Job Description:

Start by carefully reviewing the job description and highlighting the key responsibilities, qualifications, and skills required for the role. Pay attention to specific language used in the description, as this can give you clues about the types of questions you may be asked.

2: Match Your Experience:

Compare your own skills, experiences, and qualifications to the requirements outlined in the job description. Identify examples from your past experiences that demonstrate your ability to meet these requirements.

3: Common Interview Questions:

Research common interview questions for the type of role you are applying for. For example, if you are interviewing for a customer service position, you may be asked about your experience handling difficult customers or resolving conflicts.

4: Behavioral Questions:

Anticipate behavioral questions that ask you to provide examples of past experiences. These questions often start with phrases like "Tell me about a time when..." or "Give me an example of..." Prepare specific, detailed examples that demonstrate your skills and qualifications.

5: Technical Questions:

If the job requires specific technical skills, be prepared to answer questions that test your knowledge in these areas. Review any relevant technical concepts or skills to ensure you can confidently discuss them during the interview.

6: Role-specific Questions:

Consider questions that are specific to the role or industry. For example, if you are interviewing for a marketing position, you may be asked about your experience with digital marketing strategies or campaign analytics.

7: Prepare Responses:

Based on your anticipation of potential questions, prepare thoughtful, concise responses that highlight your qualifications and experiences. Practice these responses to ensure they are clear and impactful.

By anticipating questions based on the job requirements, you can effectively prepare for your interview and demonstrate to the interviewer that you are well-suited for the role. This can increase your chances of success and help you stand out as a strong candidate.

Chapter 2

During the Interview

A: Body Language and Non-Verbal Communication

Body language and non-verbal communication play a significant role in how you are perceived during a job interview. Your body language can convey confidence, professionalism, and engagement, which are all important qualities that employers look for in candidates. Here's how you can effectively use body language and non-verbal communication during an interview:

1: Eye Contact:

Maintain good eye contact with the interviewer(s) throughout the interview. This shows that you are attentive and interested in the conversation. Avoiding eye contact can make you appear disinterested or untrustworthy.

2: Posture:

Sit up straight and avoid slouching. Good posture conveys confidence and professionalism. Slouching can make you appear lazy or uninterested.

3: Hand Gestures:

Use natural hand gestures to emphasize your points, but avoid excessive or distracting movements. Gesturing can help convey enthusiasm and engagement.

4: Facial Expressions:

Smile appropriately and use facial expressions to show interest and understanding. A warm smile can help create a positive impression.

5: Mirroring:

Pay attention to the interviewer's body language and try to subtly mirror their gestures and posture. Mirroring can create a sense of rapport and connection.

6: Personal Space:

Respect the interviewer's personal space and maintain an appropriate distance. Invading personal space can make the interviewer uncomfortable.

7: Listening:

Use non-verbal cues such as nodding and maintaining eye contact to show that you are actively listening to the interviewer. This demonstrates your interest in the conversation.

8: Avoiding Negative Cues:

Avoid negative body language such as crossing your arms, fidgeting, or tapping your feet. These gestures can convey nervousness or defensiveness.

9: Confidence:

Project confidence through your body language, even if you are feeling nervous. Stand or sit tall, make eye contact, and speak clearly and confidently.

10: Practice:

Practice your body language in front of a mirror or with a friend to ensure that you are conveying the right signals. Pay attention to your posture, gestures, and facial expressions.

By paying attention to your body language and non-verbal communication, you can enhance your interview performance and make a positive impression on the interviewer. Practice these techniques to ensure that your body language aligns with the impression you want to convey during the interview.

B: Active Listening

Active listening is a crucial skill during a job interview, as it demonstrates your interest in the role and your ability to understand and respond to information effectively. Active listening involves more than just hearing words; it involves fully engaging with the speaker and processing the information to provide thoughtful responses. Here's how you can practice active listening during an interview:

1: Give Your Full Attention:

Focus on the interviewer and avoid distractions such as checking your phone or looking around the room. Show that you are fully engaged in the conversation.

2: Maintain Eye Contact:

Make regular eye contact with the interviewer to show that you are listening and interested in what they are saying. This also helps build rapport and connection.

3: Nod and Use Encouraging Gestures:

Use nods and other non-verbal cues to show that you are listening and understanding. This encourages the interviewer to continue speaking.

4: Paraphrase and Repeat:

Occasionally paraphrase what the interviewer has said to ensure that you have understood correctly. This shows that you are actively processing the information.

5: Ask Clarifying Questions:

If something is unclear, don't hesitate to ask for clarification. This shows that you are paying attention and want to ensure that you understand the information correctly.

6: Avoid Interrupting:

Wait for the interviewer to finish speaking before responding. Interrupting can be seen as rude and can disrupt the flow of the conversation.

7: Reflect on What You've Heard:

Take a moment to reflect on the information before responding. This shows that you are thoughtful in your responses and not just reacting impulsively.

8: Respond Thoughtfully:

When it's your turn to speak, respond thoughtfully and directly to the questions or comments made by the interviewer. Use the information you've gathered through active listening to inform your responses.

9: Show Empathy:

If the interviewer is discussing a challenge or issue, show empathy and understanding. This can help build rapport and show that you are empathetic and compassionate.

10: Practice Active Listening Skills:

Practice active listening skills in your daily interactions to improve your ability to listen effectively during the interview.

By practicing active listening during a job interview, you can demonstrate your communication skills, empathy, and ability to engage with others effectively. This can help you make a positive impression on the interviewer and increase your chances of success.

C: Clarifying Questions

Clarifying questions are an important tool during a job interview to ensure that you fully understand the information provided and can respond effectively. Clarifying questions help you gather more details, demonstrate your interest in the role, and show that you are engaged in the conversation. Here's how you can use clarifying questions during an interview:

1: Seeking Specifics:

If the interviewer mentions a project or task, ask for specific details such as the scope, timeline, and goals. This shows that you are interested in the specifics of the role.

2: Understanding Expectations:

Clarify the expectations for the role, including key responsibilities, reporting structure, and performance metrics. This helps you understand what is expected of you if you are hired.

3: Seeking Examples:

If the interviewer mentions a skill or experience they are looking for, ask for examples of how that skill or experience is used in the role. This helps you understand the context in which the skill is required.

4: Clarifying Company Culture:

Ask about the company's culture, values, and work environment to ensure that it aligns with your own values and preferences. This shows that you are considering the cultural fit as well.

5: Understanding the Interview Process:

Clarify the next steps in the interview process, including timelines and expectations. This helps you prepare for what comes next and shows that you are proactive in managing the interview process.

6: Seeking Feedback:

If you are unsure about how your skills or experience align with the role, ask for feedback. This shows that you are open to feedback and willing to improve.

7: Showing Engagement:

Asking clarifying questions throughout the interview shows that you are actively engaged in the conversation and interested in learning more about the role and the company.

8: Avoiding Misunderstandings:

Clarifying questions help avoid misunderstandings and ensure that you and the interviewer are on the same page.

9: Demonstrating Critical Thinking:

Asking thoughtful clarifying questions demonstrates your ability to think critically and analyze information effectively.

10: Showing Interest:

Asking clarifying questions shows that you are genuinely interested in the role and the company, which can leave a positive impression on the interviewer.

By using clarifying questions during a job interview, you can ensure that you have a clear understanding of the role and the company, allowing you to respond effectively and demonstrate your suitability for the position.

Chapter 3

After the Interview

A: Sending a Thank You Note

Sending a thank-you note after a job interview is a professional courtesy that can leave a positive impression on the interviewer and potentially increase your chances of being hired. A well-crafted thank-you note can demonstrate your appreciation for the opportunity, reiterate your interest in the position, and highlight your qualifications. Here's how you can effectively send a thank-you note:

1: Timing:

Send your thank-you note within 24 hours of the interview to ensure that it is timely. This shows that you are proactive and eager about the opportunity.

2: Personalization:

Address the thank-you note to the interviewer(s) by name. If you interviewed with multiple people, consider sending personalized notes to each individual.

3: Express Gratitude:

Start by expressing your gratitude for the opportunity to interview for the position. Be sincere and specific about what you appreciated about the interview experience.

4: Reiterate Interest:

Reiterate your interest in the position and the company. Mention specific aspects of the role or the company that excite you and align with your career goals.

5: Highlight Qualifications:

Briefly highlight your qualifications and how they make you a strong candidate for the position. This is an opportunity to reinforce your fit for the role.

6: Address Concerns or Follow-up:

If there were any concerns raised during the interview or if there are additional details you wish to provide, address them in your thank-you note. This shows that you are proactive and attentive to details.

7: Professional Tone:

Maintain a professional tone throughout the thank-you note. Avoid using overly casual language or humor.

8: Proofread:

Before sending the thank-you note, proofread it carefully to ensure that there are no grammatical or spelling errors. A well-written note reflects positively on your attention to detail.

9: Use Email or Handwritten Note:

Email is the most common method for sending thank-you notes, as it is fast and convenient. However, if you feel that a handwritten note would be more personal or appropriate, you can opt for that instead.

10: Follow-up:

If you haven't heard back from the interviewer after sending your thank-you note, it is appropriate to follow up after a week or so to reiterate your interest and inquire about the status of the hiring process.

By sending a well-crafted thank-you note after a job interview, you can leave a positive impression on the interviewer and demonstrate your professionalism and enthusiasm for the position.

B: Following Up

Following up after a job interview is an important step in the hiring process. It allows you to express continued interest in the position, reiterate your qualifications, and keep yourself top of mind for the interviewer. Here's how you can effectively follow up after a job interview:

1: Timing:

Send a follow-up email or message within a week of the interview. This shows that you are proactive and interested in the position without being too pushy.

2: Express Appreciation:

Begin your follow-up message by expressing your appreciation for the opportunity to interview for the position. Thank the interviewer for their time and consideration.

3: Reiterate Interest:

Reiterate your interest in the position and the company. Mention specific aspects of the role or the company that excite you and align with your career goals.

4: Highlight Qualifications:

Briefly remind the interviewer of your qualifications and how they make you a strong candidate for the position. Focus on the key skills and experiences that are most relevant to the role.

5: Address Concerns or Follow-up:

If there were any concerns raised during the interview or if there are additional details you wish to provide, address them in your follow-up message. This shows that you are attentive and proactive.

6: Ask About Next Steps:

Politely inquire about the next steps in the hiring process. This shows that you are eager to move forward and allows you to get a sense of the timeline for the decision.

7: Maintain Professionalism:

Keep your follow-up message professional and courteous. Avoid being overly familiar or demanding.

8: Proofread:

Before sending your follow-up message, proofread it carefully to ensure that there are no grammatical or spelling errors. A well-written message reflects positively on your attention to detail.

9: Use Email:

Email is the most common method for following up after a job interview, as it is fast and convenient. Use the same email address you used for your application to ensure it reaches the right person.

10: Be Patient:

After sending your follow-up message, be patient and wait for a response. Hiring processes can take time, so give the interviewer ample time to get back to you.

By following up after a job interview, you can demonstrate your continued interest in the position and keep yourself on the interviewer's radar. This proactive approach can help you stand out as a strong candidate for the role.

C: Reflecting on the Experience for Future Interviews

Reflecting on your interview experience can be a valuable step in preparing for future interviews and improving your interview skills. It allows you to identify areas of strength and areas for improvement, which can help you perform better in future interviews. Here's how you can effectively reflect on your interview experience:

1: Evaluate Your Performance:

Consider how well you answered the interview questions, how you presented yourself, and how you handled different aspects of the interview. Identify what went well and what could have been improved.

2: Review Feedback:

If you received feedback from the interviewer or from others, take it into consideration. Reflect on the feedback and think about how you can apply it to improve your interview skills.

3: Identify Areas for Improvement:

Based on your evaluation and feedback, identify specific areas where you can improve. This could include improving your responses to certain types of questions, enhancing your body language, or refining your overall interview technique.

4: Consider Your Preparation:

Think about how well you prepared for the interview. Did you research the company thoroughly? Did you practice your responses to common interview questions? Reflect on how your preparation affected your performance.

5: Reflect on Your Goals:

Consider whether the interview experience aligned with your career goals and aspirations. Reflect on whether the role and the company are a good fit for you based on the interview experience.

6: Set Goals for Improvement:

Based on your reflection, set specific goals for improvement. This could include practicing your responses to certain types of questions, working on your body language, or enhancing your overall interview strategy.

7: Seek Feedback:

If possible, seek feedback from the interviewer or from others who were involved in the interview process. This can provide valuable insights into areas where you can improve.

8: Practice and Prepare:

Use your reflection to guide your practice and preparation for future interviews. Focus on improving in the areas where you identified the need for improvement.

9: Stay Positive:

While it's important to reflect on areas for improvement, it's also important to stay positive and confident. Use your reflection as a learning opportunity to improve your interview skills.

10: Stay Motivated:

Use your reflection as motivation to continue improving your interview skills. Remember that each interview is a learning experience that can help you grow and develop as a candidate.

By reflecting on your interview experience, you can gain valuable insights that can help you improve your interview skills and perform better in future interviews. Use your reflection to set goals for improvement and to stay motivated in your job search.

Chapter 4

100 Interview Questions and Answers

A: Behavioral Questions

Behavioral questions are a common type of interview question that ask you to provide specific examples from your past experiences to demonstrate your skills and abilities. These questions are designed to assess how you have handled various situations in the past and how you are likely to behave in similar situations in the future. Here's how you can effectively respond to behavioral questions:

1: Understand the STAR Method:

The STAR method (Situation, Task, Action, Result) is a helpful framework for answering behavioral questions. Start by describing the Situation or Task, then explain the

Action you took, and finally, describe the Result or outcome of your actions.

2: Prepare Examples:

Before the interview, review the job description and identify key skills and competencies required for the role. Prepare examples from your past experiences that demonstrate these skills, using the STAR method to structure your responses.

3: Be Specific:

When answering behavioral questions, be specific and provide detailed examples. Use concrete examples from your past experiences to illustrate your points.

4: Highlight Your Skills:

Use behavioral questions as an opportunity to highlight your skills and abilities. Focus on examples that demonstrate your ability to problem-solve, communicate effectively, work in a team, and other relevant skills for the role.

5: Stay Positive:

When describing challenging situations, focus on how you effectively handled the challenge and the positive outcome that resulted from your actions.

6: Tailor Your Responses:

Tailor your responses to the specific job and company you are interviewing with. Use examples that are relevant to the role and demonstrate your fit for the position.

7: Practice Your Responses:

Practice answering behavioral questions before the interview to ensure that you are comfortable with the STAR method and can provide clear, concise, and relevant examples.

8: Listen Carefully:

Pay attention to the interviewer's questions and make sure you understand what they are asking for. If you are unsure, ask for clarification before responding.

9: Be Honest:

Be honest in your responses and avoid exaggerating or fabricating examples. Interviewers can often tell when a candidate is not being genuine.

10: Follow Up:

After providing your example, you can often add a follow-up about what you learned or how you would approach the situation differently now, showing growth and reflection.

By effectively answering behavioral questions, you can demonstrate your qualifications and suitability for the role, increasing your chances of success in the interview process.

B: Situational Questions

Situational questions are commonly used in interviews to assess how you would handle specific scenarios or challenges that are likely to arise in the role you are applying for. These questions are hypothetical and require you to use your knowledge, skills, and experience to formulate a response. Here's how you can effectively respond to situational questions:

1: Understand the Question:

Listen carefully to the question and make sure you understand the situation being presented. If you are unsure, ask for clarification before responding.

2: Use the STAR Method:

Like with behavioral questions, the STAR method (Situation, Task, Action, Result) can be useful for structuring your response to situational questions. Describe the Situation or Task, explain the Action you would take, and discuss the Result you would expect.

3: Tailor Your Response:

Tailor your response to the specific situation presented in the question. Draw on relevant examples from your past experiences that demonstrate your ability to handle similar situations.

4: Be Specific:

Provide specific details in your response, including the actions you would take and the outcomes you would expect. This demonstrates your ability to think critically and problem-solve effectively.

5: Focus on Your Approach:

When answering situational questions, focus on explaining your thought process and approach to the situation. This gives the interviewer insight into how you would handle challenges in the role.

6: Highlight Relevant Skills:

Use situational questions as an opportunity to highlight your relevant skills and competencies. For example, if the question is about conflict resolution, emphasize your ability to communicate effectively and find mutually acceptable solutions.

7: Stay Positive:

Even if the situation presented in the question is challenging, maintain a positive attitude in your response. Focus on how you would approach the situation proactively and professionally.

8: Be Realistic:

While it's important to demonstrate problem-solving skills, make sure your response is realistic and practical. Avoid overly ambitious or unrealistic solutions.

9: Show Adaptability:

Demonstrate your ability to adapt to different situations by considering different approaches or solutions to the problem presented in the question.

10: Practice Your Responses:

Practice answering situational questions before the interview to ensure that you can respond confidently and effectively.

By effectively answering situational questions, you can demonstrate your ability to think critically, problem-solve, and handle challenges, which are important qualities employers look for in candidates.

C: Technical Questions

Technical questions are often asked in job interviews to assess your knowledge and expertise in a specific field or skill set relevant to the job. These questions can vary widely depending on the role and industry but generally aim to evaluate your technical proficiency and problem-solving abilities. Here are some tips for effectively answering technical questions:

1: Understand the Question:

Make sure you understand the technical question being asked. If you are unsure, ask the interviewer to clarify or provide more context.

2: Be Honest:

If you don't know the answer to a technical question, it's okay to admit it. Trying to bluff your way through can backfire. Instead, focus on explaining how you would go about finding the answer or solving the problem.

3: Demonstrate Your Knowledge:

When answering technical questions, demonstrate your knowledge and expertise in the relevant area. Provide specific examples from your experience that highlight your technical skills.

4: Use Technical Jargon Appropriately:

Use technical jargon and terminology that are appropriate for the industry and the level of the interviewer. Avoid using overly complex language that may confuse the interviewer.

5: Provide Detailed Responses:

When answering technical questions, provide detailed and comprehensive responses. Explain the reasoning behind your answer and how you arrived at your conclusion.

6: Showcase Problem-Solving Skills:

Use technical questions as an opportunity to showcase your problem-solving skills. Explain your approach to solving technical problems and how you would troubleshoot issues.

7: Stay Up-to-Date:

Demonstrate that you stay up-to-date with the latest trends and developments in your field. Mention any relevant certifications, courses, or training you have completed.

8: Be Prepared:

Before the interview, review the job description and the technical skills required for the role. Prepare examples from your past experiences that demonstrate your proficiency in these areas.

9: Practice Coding Problems:

If the role requires programming or coding skills, practice coding problems and algorithms to ensure you are prepared for technical coding questions.

10: Seek Clarification:

If you are unsure about a technical question, don't hesitate to ask for clarification. It's better to ask for clarification than to provide an incorrect or incomplete answer.

By effectively answering technical questions, you can demonstrate your technical expertise and suitability for the role, increasing your chances of success in the interview process.

D: Common Questions

Common questions in job interviews are those that are frequently asked across different industries and roles. While the specific questions may vary, common themes often include inquiries about your background, skills, and qualifications, as well as your interest in the role and company. Here are some tips for effectively answering common interview questions:

1: Tell Me About Yourself:

This is often the first question in an interview and is an opportunity to provide a brief overview of your background, experience, and qualifications. Keep your answer concise and focus on relevant information.

2: What Are Your Strengths and Weaknesses:

When discussing your strengths, highlight qualities that are relevant to the role and supported by examples from your experience. For weaknesses, choose a genuine area for improvement and explain how you are working to address it.

3: Why Are You Interested in This Position/Company:

Demonstrate your interest in the role and company by discussing how your skills and experience align with the job requirements and how you see yourself contributing to the company's goals.

4: Where Do You See Yourself in Five Years:

Show that you have thought about your career goals and how this position fits into your long-term plans. Be realistic and focus on how you hope to grow and develop within the company.

5: Tell Me About a Challenge You've Overcome:

Use the STAR method (Situation, Task, Action, Result) to structure your response, focusing on a specific challenge, the actions you took to overcome it, and the positive outcome.

6: Why Should We Hire You:

Highlight your unique qualifications and what sets you apart from other candidates. Focus on how your skills and experience make you a strong fit for the role and how you can contribute to the company's success.

7: How Do You Handle Stress/Pressure:

Discuss strategies you use to stay calm and focused under pressure, such as prioritizing tasks, seeking support from colleagues, or taking breaks when needed.

8: Tell Me About a Time You Demonstrated Leadership:

Even if you haven't held a formal leadership role, think of a situation where you took initiative, motivated others, or achieved a positive outcome through your actions.

9: What Do You Know About Our Company:

Demonstrate your knowledge of the company by discussing its mission, values, products or services, and any recent news or developments that are relevant to the role.

10: Do You Have Any Questions for Us:

Prepare thoughtful questions that demonstrate your interest in the role and company. Ask about the company culture, opportunities for growth and development, or specific aspects of the role that were not covered in the interview.

By preparing and practicing your responses to these common interview questions, you can showcase your qualifications and suitability for the role, increasing your chances of success in the interview process.

E: Unexpected Questions

Unexpected questions in interviews are designed to gauge your creativity, problem-solving skills, and ability to think on your feet. These questions do not have a right or wrong answer but are intended to see how you approach a challenge or unfamiliar situation. Here are some tips for handling unexpected questions:

1: Stay Calm:

Keep your composure and take a moment to think before responding. It's okay to pause and gather your thoughts.

2: Clarify the Question:

If you're unsure about the question or need more information, don't hesitate to ask for clarification. This shows that you are thoughtful and detail-oriented.

3: Use the STAR Method:

If possible, try to structure your response using the STAR method (Situation, Task, Action, Result) to provide a clear and concise answer.

4: Be Creative:

Use unexpected questions as an opportunity to showcase your creativity and innovative thinking. Think outside the box and consider different perspectives or approaches to the question.

5: Stay Relevant:

While unexpected questions may be unconventional, try to keep your response relevant to the job and company. Tie your answer back to your skills or experiences whenever possible.

6: Stay Positive:

Even if you find the question challenging, approach it with a positive attitude. Use humor or storytelling to make your answer engaging.

7: Relate to Your Skills:

If the question seems unrelated to the job, find a way to connect it to your skills or experiences. For example, you could relate it to a past project or problem you've solved.

8: Be Honest:

It's okay to admit if you don't know the answer to an unexpected question. Use the opportunity to explain how you would approach finding a solution or learning more about the topic.

9: Practice Makes Perfect:

While you can't predict every unexpected question, practicing responding to unusual or challenging questions can help you feel more comfortable and prepared.

10: Follow Up:

If you feel your initial response was not as strong as it could have been, consider following up with a more thoughtful answer or additional information.

By approaching unexpected questions with a positive attitude and using them as an opportunity to showcase your skills and creativity, you can impress interviewers and stand out as a candidate.

Question 1: Tell me about yourself?

"Tell me about yourself?" is often the first question asked in an interview, and it's your opportunity to make a strong first impression. Here's how you can approach this question:

I: Keep it Professional:

Start by mentioning your name and a brief professional background. Highlight key experiences or accomplishments that are relevant to the job you're interviewing for.

II: Focus on Relevant Experience:

Tailor your response to emphasize experiences and skills that directly relate to the position. Mentioning your most recent job role or a significant achievement can be a good start.

III: Highlight Your Strengths:

Talk about your strengths and how they align with the job requirements. Use specific examples to demonstrate your skills and abilities.

IV: Show Enthusiasm:

Express your enthusiasm for the role and the company. Mention why you're interested in the position and how you believe you can contribute to the organization's goals.

V: Keep it Concise:

While you want to provide enough information to make a strong impression, avoid rambling or providing unnecessary details. Aim to keep your answer to about 2-3 minutes.

Example Answer:

"Sure, my name is [Your Name], and I have a background in [Your Field/Industry]. I recently worked as a [Your Most Recent Job Title], where I [Briefly Describe Your Responsibilities or Achievements]. I'm particularly excited about this opportunity at [Company Name] because [Reasons Why You're Interested], and I believe my skills in [Your Skills] make me a strong fit for the role. I'm looking forward to discussing how I can contribute to your team."

Remember to practice your answer beforehand to ensure you're able to deliver it confidently and succinctly.

Question 2: Why do you want this job?

"Why do you want this job?" is a common interview question that allows you to demonstrate your interest in the position and the company. Here's how you can approach this question:

I: Research the Company:

Start by mentioning specific aspects of the company that appeal to you, such as its culture, values, or reputation. This shows that you've done your homework and are genuinely interested in the organization.

II: Align Your Goals:

Explain how the job aligns with your career goals and aspirations. Mention how the role will help you grow professionally and develop new skills.

III: Highlight Your Fit:

Emphasize why you're a good fit for the position based on your skills, experiences, and interests. Talk about how your background makes you uniquely qualified for the role.

IV: Show Enthusiasm:

Express your enthusiasm for the opportunity and the company. Mention why you're excited about the role and how you believe you can contribute to the organization's success.

V: Be Honest:

Provide genuine reasons for why you want the job. Avoid generic answers and instead, focus on specific aspects of the role or company that appeal to you.

Example Answer:

"I'm excited about this job at [Company Name] because I've been following your work in [Industry/Field], and I'm impressed by your commitment to [Specific Value or Goal]. I believe my background in [Your Field/Industry] makes me a strong fit for the role, and I'm eager to contribute my skills to help [Company Name] achieve its objectives. Additionally, I'm excited about the opportunity to [Specific Goal or Responsibility of the Job], which aligns perfectly with my career aspirations."

By providing a thoughtful and genuine answer to this question, you can demonstrate your enthusiasm for the role and showcase how you're a strong fit for the position.

Question 3: How did you hear about this position?

"How did you hear about this position?" is a straightforward question that allows the interviewer to understand how you became aware of the job opening. Here's how you can approach this question:

I: Be Honest:

Provide an honest answer about how you learned about the job opening. Whether it was through a job board, company website, referral, or networking event, be truthful in your response.

II: Highlight Your Interest:

Use this question as an opportunity to show your interest in the position and the company. Mention any specific aspects of the job or organization that caught your attention and motivated you to apply.

III: Connect it to Your Career Goals:

If relevant, explain how this position aligns with your career goals and why you are excited about the opportunity.

IV: Show Appreciation:

If you learned about the job through a referral or networking contact, express your gratitude for their help in connecting you with the opportunity.

Example Answer:

"I heard about this position through [Source], and I was immediately drawn to it because of [Reason]. I've been following [Company Name] for some time and have been impressed by [Specific Aspect of Company]. When I saw the job posting, I knew it was a perfect fit for my skills and career goals. I'm excited about the opportunity to contribute to such a great company."

By providing a concise and honest answer to this question, you can demonstrate your interest in the position and the company, as well as show how you align with the organization's goals and values.

Question 4: Tell me something that is not on your CV?

"Tell me something that is not on your CV?" is a question that allows you to share more about yourself beyond what is listed on your resume. Here's how you can approach this question:

I: Choose Relevant Information:

Select something that is relevant to the job or that showcases your skills or personality in a positive light. For example, you could talk about a hobby or interest that demonstrates your creativity, leadership, or problem-solving skills.

II: Make it Personal but Professional:

While you can share personal information, such as a hobby or interest, make sure it's something that is appropriate for a professional setting. Avoid sharing overly personal details that are unrelated to the job.

III: Highlight Your Fit for the Role:

Use this opportunity to further demonstrate why you are a good fit for the role. For example, if the job requires strong communication skills, you could talk about your experience volunteering as a public speaker for a charity organization.

IV: Keep it Concise:

Be mindful of the interviewer's time and keep your answer concise and to the point. Aim to share something interesting about yourself in just a few sentences.

Example Answer:

"One thing that is not on my CV is my passion for photography. In my free time, I enjoy capturing moments and telling stories through my photographs. I believe this hobby has helped me develop my creativity and attention to detail, which are skills that I bring to my work as a [Your Profession]."

By providing a thoughtful and relevant answer to this question, you can showcase another dimension of yourself to the interviewer and demonstrate how your personal interests and skills can benefit the role.

Question 5: Why do you want to leave your current job?

"Why do you want to leave your current job?" is a question that requires a delicate balance of honesty and professionalism. Here's how you can approach this question:

I: Focus on Growth:

Emphasize your desire for professional growth and new challenges. Explain how the role you're interviewing for aligns better with your long-term career goals.

II: Highlight Positive Reasons:

Avoid speaking negatively about your current job or employer. Instead, focus on positive reasons for wanting to leave, such as seeking a new opportunity for advancement or a better cultural fit.

III: Discuss Career Goals:

Use this question as an opportunity to discuss your career goals and how the new position aligns with them. Highlight how the new role will help you further develop your skills and expertise.

IV: Be Honest but Tactful:

If there are specific challenges in your current job that have led you to seek new opportunities, be honest but tactful in how you discuss them. Focus on the positive aspects of the new role rather than the negative aspects of your current job.

Example Answer:

"I've enjoyed my time at my current job and have learned a lot, but I feel that I have reached a point where I'm ready for new challenges and opportunities for growth. I'm excited about the possibility of joining your team because [Reasons Why New Job is Appealing], and I believe this role aligns better with my long-term career goals."

By providing a positive and forward-looking answer to this question, you can demonstrate your professionalism and enthusiasm for the new opportunity while also addressing the reasons for wanting to leave your current job.

Question 6: Why are there gaps in your employment?

"Why are there gaps in your employment?" is a question that may come up if you have periods of time where you were not employed. Here's how you can approach this question:

I: Be Honest:

Explain the reasons for the gaps in your employment honestly. Whether it was due to personal reasons, a layoff, or a career break, provide a truthful explanation.

II: Highlight Relevant Activities:

If you were engaged in any activities during the gaps, such as volunteering, freelancing, or taking courses, mention them. This shows that you were productive during those periods.

III: Focus on the Positive:

Emphasize what you learned or gained from the gap in employment. For example, you may have developed new skills, gained valuable experience, or had time to reassess your career goals.

IV: Address the Gap Proactively:

If the gap was due to a specific reason, such as a layoff or health issue, address it proactively and explain how you have addressed or overcome the challenge.

V: Reassure the Interviewer:

Assure the interviewer that the gap in your employment will not affect your ability to perform the job effectively.

Highlight your enthusiasm and readiness to re-enter the workforce.

Example Answer:

"I had a gap in my employment due to [Reason for Gap], during which time I [Activities or Steps Taken During Gap]. This experience taught me [What You Learned or Gained], and I'm now eager to apply my skills and experience in a new role. I'm excited about the opportunity at your company because [Reasons Why New Job is Appealing], and I believe my background makes me a strong fit for the position."

By addressing the gap in your employment proactively and focusing on the positive aspects of your experience, you can reassure the interviewer that you are a qualified candidate despite any gaps in your work history.

Question 7: Why should we hire you?

"Why should we hire you?" is a question that allows you to showcase your qualifications and explain why you are the best candidate for the job. Here's how you can approach this question:

I: Highlight Your Skills and Experience:

Focus on the skills, experiences, and qualifications that make you uniquely suited for the position. Highlight specific achievements or accomplishments that demonstrate your abilities.

II: Align with the Job Requirements:

Discuss how your skills and experiences align with the requirements of the job. Explain how you can contribute to the company and help achieve its goals.

III: Show Your Enthusiasm:

Express your enthusiasm for the role and the company. Demonstrate your passion for the industry and your eagerness to make a positive impact.

IV: Provide Concrete Examples:

Use specific examples from your past experiences to illustrate why you are the best candidate for the job. Highlight how you have successfully handled similar responsibilities or challenges in the past.

V: Be Confident but Humble:

While it's important to showcase your strengths, be careful not to come across as arrogant. Express your confidence in your abilities while acknowledging that you are always willing to learn and grow.

Example Answer:

"I believe that my combination of [Your Skills/Experience] makes me a perfect fit for this role. In my previous position at [Previous Company], I was able to [Specific Achievement or Accomplishment]. I'm confident that I can bring the same level of success to your team. I'm particularly excited about the opportunity at your company because [Reasons Why New Job is Appealing], and I believe that my background in

[Your Field/Industry] uniquely qualifies me for this position."

By providing a compelling argument for why you are the best candidate for the job and demonstrating your enthusiasm for the role and the company, you can make a strong case for why the interviewer should hire you.

Question 8: Where do you see yourself in five years?

"Where do you see yourself in five years?" is a question that aims to understand your career goals and aspirations. Here's how you can approach this question:

I: Be Realistic:

Your answer should be realistic and achievable. Avoid making grandiose statements or unrealistic goals.

II: Align with the Company:

Tailor your answer to align with the company's goals and the potential career path within the organization.

III: Demonstrate Ambition:

Show that you are ambitious and have a clear vision for your career growth. Mention specific goals or milestones you hope to achieve in the next five years.

IV: Show Adaptability:

While it's good to have a plan, also demonstrate that you are open to new opportunities and willing to adapt to changes in the industry or organization.

V: Focus on Personal Growth:

Mention how you hope to grow both professionally and personally in the next five years. Talk about the skills you hope to develop and how you plan to continue learning and growing.

Example Answer:

"In five years, I see myself taking on more leadership responsibilities and possibly managing a team. I'm excited about the opportunity to grow within this company and contribute to its success. I also hope to further develop my skills in [Your Field/Industry] and stay updated with the latest industry trends and technologies. Ultimately, I want to be in a position where I can make a significant impact and help drive the company's growth and success."

By providing a thoughtful and realistic answer to this question, you can demonstrate your ambition, commitment to growth, and alignment with the company's goals, making you a strong candidate for the position.

Question 9: Where do you see yourself in five years?

"Where do you see yourself in five years?" is a common interview question that allows the interviewer to gauge your long-term career goals and aspirations. Here's how you can approach this question:

I: Be Specific but Flexible:

Provide a specific answer that demonstrates your ambition and vision for your career, but also be open to the possibility of change and new opportunities.

II: Align with the Company:

Tailor your answer to align with the company's goals and values. Show that you have thought about how your career goals fit into the larger context of the organization.

III: Focus on Growth:

Emphasize your desire for personal and professional growth. Mention how you plan to develop your skills and expertise over the next five years.

IV: Show Commitment:

Express your commitment to the company and your interest in growing with the organization. Mention how you see yourself contributing to the company's success in the long term.

V: Be Realistic:

While it's good to be ambitious, make sure your goals are realistic and achievable within the given timeframe.

Example Answer:

"In five years, I see myself as a senior [Your Current Role] with a strong track record of success in [Your Field/Industry]. I plan to further develop my leadership skills and take on more challenging projects that allow me to make a significant impact within the organization. I'm excited about the opportunity to grow with this company and contribute to its continued success."

By providing a thoughtful and well-considered answer to this question, you can demonstrate your ambition, commitment, and alignment with the company's goals, making you a strong candidate for the position.

Question 10: Describe yourself in 3 words?

"Describe yourself in three words?" is a question that requires you to summarize your key qualities or characteristics in a concise and impactful way. Here's how you can approach this question:

I: Choose Relevant Words:

Select words that are relevant to the job and reflect your strengths and qualities that align with the position.

II: Be Honest and Authentic:

Choose words that truly represent who you are as a person and a professional. Avoid using buzzwords or generic terms that could apply to anyone.

III: Provide Examples:

If possible, provide brief examples or anecdotes that illustrate each of the three words you choose. This can help the interviewer get a better understanding of how you embody these qualities.

IV: Keep it Professional:

While it's okay to include personal qualities, focus primarily on professional attributes that are relevant to the job.

V: Be Positive:

Choose words that have positive connotations and highlight your strengths rather than weaknesses.

Example Answer:

"Adaptable, determined, and collaborative. I have a track record of adapting to new situations and challenges, staying determined to achieve my goals, and working collaboratively with others to achieve success. These qualities have helped me succeed in my previous roles and I believe they will continue to serve me well in future endeavors."

By providing a thoughtful and genuine answer to this question, you can demonstrate your self-awareness, professionalism, and suitability for the job.

Question 11: What didn't you like about your last job?

"What didn't you like about your last job?" is a question that requires you to discuss the aspects of your previous job that you found challenging or dissatisfying. Here's how you can approach this question:

I: Be Diplomatic:

Avoid speaking negatively about your previous employer or colleagues. Instead, focus on the specific aspects of the job itself that you found challenging.

II: Focus on Growth:

Frame your answer in a way that highlights your desire for professional growth and development. For example, you could mention that you found the lack of opportunities for advancement challenging.

III: Highlight Your Values:

If the aspects you didn't like about your last job are related to your values or work ethic, you can mention them. For example, if you value collaboration and your previous job was very individual-focused, you could mention that as a challenge.

IV: Show Adaptability:

Mention how you tried to address or overcome the challenges you faced in your last job. This demonstrates your ability to adapt and problem-solve in difficult situations.

V: Be Concise:

Keep your answer brief and focused on the key points. Avoid going into too much detail or dwelling on negative aspects.

Example Answer:

"One of the challenges I faced in my last job was the lack of opportunities for professional growth and advancement. While I enjoyed the work itself and the team I was a part of, I found that after a certain point, there were limited opportunities to take on new challenges or advance within the organization. This is one of the reasons I'm excited about the opportunity here, as I see it as a chance to continue growing and advancing in my career."

By providing a thoughtful and diplomatic answer to this question, you can demonstrate your ability to reflect on past experiences, identify areas for improvement, and show your motivation for seeking new opportunities.

Question 12: What are your greatest strengths?

"What are your greatest strengths?" is a question that allows you to showcase your skills, qualities, and attributes that make you a strong candidate for the job. Here's how you can approach this question:

I: Focus on Relevant Strengths:

Choose strengths that are relevant to the job and demonstrate your ability to excel in the role. For example, if the job requires strong communication skills, you could mention that as one of your strengths.

II: Provide Examples:

Back up your strengths with specific examples from your past experiences. This helps to illustrate how you have demonstrated these strengths in real-life situations.

III: Be Authentic:

Choose strengths that genuinely reflect who you are as a person and a professional. Avoid using generic or cliché strengths that could apply to anyone.

IV: Show Impact:

Explain how your strengths have contributed to your success in your previous roles. For example, if you mention that one of your strengths is problem-solving, you could mention a specific problem you solved and the positive impact it had on your team or organization.

V: Be Concise:

Keep your answer focused and concise. Highlight your top strengths and avoid listing too many or going into unnecessary detail.

Example Answer:

"One of my greatest strengths is my ability to communicate effectively with others. In my previous role, I was responsible for leading a team of individuals with diverse backgrounds and skill sets. I found that by being a clear and concise communicator, I was able to ensure that everyone was on the same page and working towards the same goals. This helped to improve overall team efficiency and morale."

By providing a thoughtful and specific answer to this question, you can demonstrate your self-awareness, confidence, and suitability for the job.

Question 13: What is your biggest weakness?

"What is your biggest weakness?" is a question that aims to assess your self-awareness and ability to reflect on areas for improvement. Here's how you can approach this question:

I: Be Honest:

Select a genuine weakness that you are actively working to improve. Avoid mentioning weaknesses that are essential to the job you're applying for or that could raise red flags.

II: Show Growth and Improvement:

Discuss steps you have taken to address this weakness. This demonstrates your willingness to learn and grow professionally.

III: Focus on Professional Weaknesses:

Keep your answer focused on weaknesses that are related to your professional skills or abilities. Avoid mentioning personal weaknesses that are not relevant to the job.

IV: Turn it Into a Strength:

Frame your weakness in a way that shows how it can be a strength in certain situations. For example, if you struggle with delegating tasks, you could mention that you are working on improving your delegation skills, but you also mention that you are detail-oriented and prefer to ensure tasks are done correctly.

V: Keep it Relevant:

Choose a weakness that is relevant to the job you're applying for. For example, if the job requires strong organizational skills, you could mention that time management is an area you're working on improving.

Example Answer:

"One of my biggest weaknesses is that I can be overly critical of my own work. I tend to set very high standards for myself, which can sometimes lead to feelings of dissatisfaction, even when I've done a good job. However, I've learned to channel this drive for perfection into a positive by using it to motivate myself to continually improve and strive for excellence in everything I do."

By providing a thoughtful and honest answer to this question, you can demonstrate your self-awareness, willingness to learn, and commitment to professional growth, which are all valuable qualities in a candidate.

Question 14: What are you looking for in your next job?

"What are you looking for in your next job?" is a question that allows you to discuss your career goals, aspirations, and what you value in a work environment. Here's how you can approach this question:

I: Align with the Job:

Tailor your answer to align with the specific job and company you're interviewing with. Mention aspects of the job or company culture that appeal to you and are important for your next role.

II: Discuss Career Growth:

Express your desire for opportunities for professional development and advancement. Mention that you're looking for a job where you can grow and learn new skills.

III: Highlight Your Values:

Discuss what you value in a work environment, such as teamwork, autonomy, or a supportive culture. Explain why these aspects are important to you and how they contribute to your overall job satisfaction.

IV: Show Enthusiasm:

Express your enthusiasm for the role and the company. Mention that you're excited about the opportunity to contribute to the company's success and be a part of a dynamic team.

V: Be Specific:

Provide specific examples of what you're looking for in your next job. For example, if you value work-life balance, you could mention that you're looking for a job that offers flexibility in working hours.

Example Answer:

"In my next job, I'm looking for a role that allows me to continue to develop and grow my skills in [Your Field/Industry]. I value a supportive work environment where teamwork is encouraged, and I'm excited about the opportunity to collaborate with a diverse group of individuals. I'm also looking for a company that values professional development and offers opportunities for advancement. Overall, I'm seeking a role where I can make a meaningful contribution and continue to learn and grow."

By providing a thoughtful and tailored answer to this question, you can demonstrate your alignment with the job and company, as well as your enthusiasm and readiness to contribute to the organization's success.

Question 15: How would your friends describe you?

"How would your friends describe you?" is a question that allows you to showcase your personality and how you are perceived by others. Here's how you can approach this question:

I: Be Authentic:

Think about how your friends actually perceive you and choose words that reflect your true personality. Avoid using cliché or generic terms that could apply to anyone.

II: Focus on Positive Traits:

Highlight positive traits that are relevant to the job and reflect well on your character. For example, you could mention that your friends would describe you as reliable, friendly, or a good listener.

III: Provide Examples:

If possible, provide examples or anecdotes that illustrate the traits you mention. This can help to give the interviewer a better sense of who you are and how you interact with others.

IV: Show Self-Awareness:

Demonstrate that you have a good understanding of your own strengths and weaknesses. For example, you could mention that your friends would describe you as a perfectionist, but that you're working on finding a balance between striving for excellence and being realistic.

V: Be Concise:

Keep your answer focused and avoid going into unnecessary detail. Highlight one or two key traits that you believe are most relevant to the job and the company culture.

Example Answer:

"I believe my friends would describe me as reliable and compassionate. I always strive to be there for others when they need support, whether it's a listening ear or a helping hand. I also think they would say I have a good sense of humor and can lighten the mood in difficult situations. Overall, I value my relationships with others and try to be a positive influence in their lives."

By providing a thoughtful and authentic answer to this question, you can demonstrate your interpersonal skills, emotional intelligence, and how you might fit into the company culture.

Question 16: How do you handle pressure?

"How do you handle pressure?" is a question that assesses your ability to remain calm and focused in challenging situations. Here's how you can approach this question:

I: Describe Your Approach:

Explain your approach to handling pressure, such as staying organized, prioritizing tasks, and maintaining a positive attitude.

II: Provide Examples:

Give examples of times when you successfully managed pressure in the past. Describe the situation, the actions you took, and the outcome.

III: Highlight Your Skills:

Highlight skills that help you handle pressure, such as problem-solving, time management, and the ability to stay calm under pressure.

IV: Show Adaptability:

Demonstrate your ability to adapt to changing circumstances and handle unexpected challenges.

V: Be Honest:

Be honest about your strengths in handling pressure, but also mention areas where you are working to improve.

Example Answer:

"I handle pressure by staying organized and focused on the task at hand. I break down complex tasks into smaller, manageable steps and prioritize them based on deadlines. For example, in my previous role, we had a project with a tight deadline. I stayed calm, delegated tasks effectively, and communicated regularly with the team to ensure we met the deadline. I also make sure to take breaks and practice self-care to prevent burnout. Overall, I believe my ability to stay calm under pressure and focus on solutions has helped me successfully manage challenging situations."

Question 17: How would you deal with a conflict with a co-worker?

"How would you deal with a conflict with a co-worker?" is a question that assesses your interpersonal skills and ability to handle difficult situations in a professional manner. Here's how you can approach this question:

I: Stay Calm and Objective:

Explain that you would approach the conflict calmly and objectively, without letting emotions get in the way.

II: Listen Actively:

Describe how you would listen to the other person's perspective and try to understand their point of view.

III: Communicate Effectively:

Explain that you would communicate your own perspective clearly and respectfully, using "I" statements to express your feelings and concerns.

IV: Seek a Resolution:

Describe how you would work together with the other person to find a mutually acceptable solution to the conflict.

V: Focus on the Positive:

Emphasize that you would try to find common ground and focus on the positive aspects of your working relationship.

VI: Seek Mediation if Necessary:

Mention that if the conflict cannot be resolved directly, you would seek mediation or assistance from a supervisor or HR.

Example Answer:

"If I were to encounter a conflict with a co-worker, I would first try to address the issue directly with them in a calm and respectful manner. I would listen to their perspective and try to understand their point of view. I would then communicate my own perspective clearly and try to find common ground. If we were unable to resolve the conflict on our own, I would seek assistance from a supervisor or HR to help mediate the situation. Overall, I believe that open communication and a willingness to find a solution are key to resolving conflicts in a professional manner."

Question 18: What makes you angry or annoyed?

"What makes you angry or annoyed?" is a question that aims to understand your triggers and how you manage your emotions in the workplace. Here's how you can approach this question:

I: Be Honest but Tactful:

Select a situation that genuinely annoys or angers you, but frame it in a way that demonstrates your professionalism and ability to handle emotions.

II: Focus on Work-related Situations:

Keep your answer focused on situations that are relevant to the workplace. Avoid discussing personal pet peeves or unrelated issues.

III: Discuss Your Response:

Explain how you typically respond to situations that make you angry or annoyed. For example, you could mention that you take a moment to collect your thoughts before addressing the issue calmly and professionally.

IV: Highlight Your Problem-solving Skills:

Mention how you work to resolve the issue that caused your anger or annoyance, rather than letting it affect your work or relationships with colleagues.

V: Show Self-awareness:

Demonstrate that you are aware of your triggers and actively work to manage your emotions in a positive and constructive manner.

Example Answer:

"I find that I get annoyed when there is a lack of communication or when important information is not shared with the team. In these situations, I feel frustrated because it can impact our ability to work effectively. However, I have learned to address these issues calmly and professionally by seeking clarification and encouraging open communication within the team. I believe that clear communication is key to avoiding misunderstandings and conflicts in the workplace."

Question 19: How would you deal with a difficult customer?

"How would you deal with a difficult customer?" is a question that assesses your customer service skills and ability to handle challenging situations. Here's how you can approach this question:

I: Stay Calm and Patient:

Explain that you would remain calm and patient, even in the face of a difficult customer.

II: Listen Actively:

Describe how you would listen carefully to the customer's concerns, allowing them to fully express their issue.

III: Empathize:

Show empathy towards the customer's situation, acknowledging their feelings and demonstrating that you understand their perspective.

IV: Offer Solutions:

Explain that you would work with the customer to find a solution to their problem, offering alternatives and seeking their input.

V: Maintain Professionalism:

Emphasize that you would always maintain a professional demeanor, even if the customer becomes angry or confrontational.

VI: Seek Assistance if Necessary:

Mention that if you are unable to resolve the issue on your own, you would seek assistance from a supervisor or colleague with more authority.

Example Answer:

"If I were faced with a difficult customer, I would first listen carefully to their concerns and let them know that I understand their frustration. I would then apologize for any inconvenience they have experienced and assure them that I am committed to finding a solution. I would work with the customer to explore possible solutions, offering alternatives and seeking their input. If I am unable to resolve the issue on my own, I would escalate the matter to a supervisor or manager for further assistance. Throughout the interaction, I would maintain a calm and professional demeanor, ensuring that the customer feels heard and valued."

Question 20: Tell me about a time you provided excellent customer service?

"Tell me about a time you provided excellent customer service?" is a behavioral interview question that aims to assess your past behavior in a customer service scenario. Here's how you can approach this question using the STAR method (Situation, Task, Action, Result):

I: Situation:

Describe the situation or context in which you provided excellent customer service. Provide enough detail to paint a clear picture for the interviewer.

II: Task:

Explain the task or goal you were trying to achieve in that situation. This could be resolving a customer complaint, helping a customer make a purchase decision, or addressing a customer's inquiry.

III: Action:

Describe the specific actions you took to provide excellent customer service. Focus on the skills and qualities you demonstrated, such as empathy, problem-solving, and communication.

IV: Result:

Explain the outcome of your actions. Did the customer leave satisfied? Did you receive positive feedback? Did the situation result in a repeat customer or referral?

Example Answer:

"In my previous role as a customer service representative, I received a call from a customer who was unhappy with a product they had purchased. The customer explained that the product had not met their expectations and they were frustrated. I listened carefully to the customer's concerns and empathized with their situation. I apologized for the inconvenience and assured them that I would do everything in my power to resolve the issue.

I researched the customer's order history and found that they had been a loyal customer for several years. I offered them a full refund for the product and also provided them with a discount on their next purchase as a gesture of goodwill. The customer was delighted with the resolution and thanked me for my understanding and assistance.

As a result of my actions, the customer left satisfied and even wrote a positive review praising my exceptional customer service. This experience taught me the importance of empathy and proactive problem-solving in delivering excellent customer service."

Question 21: Tell me about a time you worked in a team?

"Tell me about a time you worked in a team?" is a common behavioral interview question that aims to assess your teamwork skills and ability to collaborate effectively with others. Here's how you can approach this question using the STAR method (Situation, Task, Action, Result):

I: Situation:

Describe the context or situation in which you worked in a team. Provide enough background information to set the stage for your story.

II: Task:

Explain the task or goal that the team was working towards. This could be a project, a problem to solve, or a target to achieve.

III: Action:

Describe the specific actions you took as part of the team. Focus on your contributions, how you interacted with team members, and any challenges you faced.

IV: Result:

Explain the outcome of the team's efforts. Did you achieve the goal? What was the impact of your teamwork? Did you learn anything from the experience?

Example Answer:

"In my previous role, I was part of a cross-functional team tasked with launching a new product. Our team consisted of members from marketing, sales, product development, and customer service. Each team member had a specific role to play in the launch process, and collaboration was key to our success.

My role in the team was to develop the marketing strategy for the product launch. I worked closely with the sales team to understand customer needs and preferences, and with the product development team to ensure that our marketing message aligned with the product's features and benefits.

One of the challenges we faced was coordinating our efforts across different departments and ensuring that everyone was aligned with the overall strategy. To address this, we held regular team meetings to update each other on our progress, share ideas, and address any issues that arose.

As a result of our teamwork, we were able to successfully launch the product on time and within budget. The product received positive feedback from customers, and sales exceeded our expectations. This experience taught me the importance of collaboration and communication in achieving common goals."

Question 22: Tell me about a challenge you had to overcome?

"Tell me about a challenge you had to overcome?" is a behavioral interview question that aims to assess your problem-solving skills and resilience in the face of adversity. Here's how you can approach this question using the STAR method (Situation, Task, Action, Result):

I: Situation:

Describe the challenge you faced. Provide enough context so the interviewer understands the scope and impact of the challenge.

II: Task:

Explain what you needed to accomplish despite the challenge. This could be a goal you needed to achieve, a deadline you needed to meet, or a problem you needed to solve.

III: Action:

Describe the specific actions you took to overcome the challenge. Focus on the steps you took, the decisions you made, and the strategies you employed.

IV: Result:

Explain the outcome of your actions. Did you successfully overcome the challenge? What did you learn from the experience?

Example Answer:

"In my previous role, I was tasked with implementing a new software system to streamline our workflow. However, halfway through the implementation process, we encountered a major technical issue that threatened to derail the entire project. The issue was complex and required a deep understanding of the software architecture to resolve.

To overcome this challenge, I first gathered all relevant information about the issue and consulted with experts in the field. I then developed a plan to address the issue, which involved a combination of software updates, configuration changes, and testing procedures.

I worked closely with the technical team to implement the plan and monitor the progress. Despite facing several setbacks and unforeseen complications, we were able to resolve the issue and successfully implement the new software system. The project was completed on time and within budget, and the new system significantly improved our workflow efficiency.

This experience taught me the importance of perseverance and problem-solving skills in overcoming challenges. It also reinforced the value of teamwork and collaboration in achieving common goals."

Question 23: Tell me about a time when you had to work closely with someone you didn't like?

"Tell me about a time when you had to work closely with someone you didn't like?" is a behavioral interview question that assesses your ability to handle interpersonal conflicts and work effectively in challenging situations. Here's how you can approach this question using the STAR method (Situation, Task, Action, Result):

I: Situation:

Describe the situation or context in which you had to work closely with someone you didn't like. Explain why you didn't get along with this person and the impact it had on your work.

II: Task:

Explain the task or goal you needed to accomplish despite your differences with this person. This could be a project you needed to complete together or a specific task you needed to work on collaboratively.

III: Action:

Describe the specific actions you took to work effectively with this person. Focus on how you managed your emotions, communicated effectively, and found common ground.

IV: Result:

Explain the outcome of your actions. Did you successfully work with this person despite your differences? What did you learn from the experience?

Example Answer:

"In a previous role, I was assigned to work closely with a colleague on a project. We had very different working styles and personalities, and we didn't always see eye to eye. This created tension between us, which made it challenging to collaborate effectively.

Despite our differences, I knew that the success of the project depended on our ability to work together. To improve our working relationship, I made an effort to understand my colleague's perspective and find common ground. I also communicated openly and respectfully, addressing any issues that arose in a constructive manner.

Over time, our working relationship improved, and we were able to collaborate more effectively. By focusing on our shared goals and finding ways to work together despite our differences, we were able to successfully complete the project. This experience taught me the importance of empathy, communication, and conflict resolution skills in building positive working relationships."

Question 24: What does success mean to you?

"What does success mean to you?" is a question that aims to understand your personal definition of success and what motivates you in your career. Here's how you can approach this question:

I: Define Success:

Begin by defining what success means to you. This could include achieving personal goals, making a positive impact, or reaching a certain level of professional accomplishment.

II: Focus on Personal Growth:

Highlight that success, for you, is not just about external achievements but also about personal growth and development. Mention that you strive to continuously learn and improve in your professional and personal life.

III: Emphasize Fulfillment:

Explain that success, to you, is also about finding fulfillment and satisfaction in your work. Mention that you are motivated by the impact your work has on others and the sense of purpose it gives you.

IV: Include Professional Achievements:

Discuss how achieving your professional goals and advancing in your career is also a part of your definition of success. Mention that you are driven to excel in your field and take on new challenges.

V: Be Authentic:

Your answer should reflect your genuine values and beliefs about success. Avoid giving a generic or cliché response and instead, focus on what truly matters to you.

Example Answer:

"To me, success is about achieving a balance between professional accomplishments and personal fulfillment. It's not just about reaching a certain position or earning a specific salary, but also about feeling fulfilled and satisfied with the work I do. Success, for me, is about making a positive impact on others, whether that's through my work, my interactions with colleagues, or my contributions to the community.

I also believe that success is a journey, not a destination. It's about continuously learning and growing, both professionally and personally. I strive to challenge myself and take on new opportunities that allow me to develop new skills and expand my knowledge.

Overall, success is about finding joy and purpose in what I do, and feeling proud of the impact I have on others and the world around me."

Question 25: What areas do you need to improve on right now?

"What areas do you need to improve on right now?" is a question that assesses your self-awareness and willingness to acknowledge areas where you can grow. Here's how you can approach this question:

I: Identify Areas for Improvement:

Think about areas where you can enhance your skills, knowledge, or behavior. This could include technical skills, soft skills, or personal habits.

II: Be Honest and Specific:

Choose one or two areas that are relevant to the job you're applying for and where you genuinely feel you can improve. Avoid mentioning generic weaknesses that are not relevant to the role.

III: Explain Your Plan:

Describe the steps you are taking or planning to take to improve in these areas. This could include taking courses, seeking mentorship, or practicing new techniques.

IV: Show Your Commitment to Growth:

Emphasize that you are actively working to improve in these areas and that you see it as an ongoing process.

V: Highlight Your Self-Awareness:

Mention that you are aware of your weaknesses and are committed to addressing them. This demonstrates maturity and a proactive attitude towards self-improvement.

Example Answer:

"One area I'm currently working on improving is my public speaking skills. While I'm comfortable speaking in front of small groups, I know that I can improve my confidence and delivery when speaking to larger audiences. To address this, I've enrolled in a public speaking course and have been practicing my presentations regularly. I've also sought feedback from colleagues and mentors to help me identify areas for improvement. I believe that improving my public speaking skills will not only benefit me professionally but also enhance my ability to communicate effectively in various settings."

Question 26: When you start a new job, how do you adapt to the different working environment?

"When you start a new job, how do you adapt to the different working environment?" is a question that assesses your adaptability and ability to thrive in new environments. Here's how you can approach this question:

I: Research and Observation:

Explain that you start by researching the company culture, values, and norms. You observe how things are done and how people interact in the new environment.

II: Building Relationships:

Emphasize the importance of building relationships with colleagues and supervisors. You make an effort to get to know your team members and establish rapport with them.

III: Learning and Development:

Mention that you focus on learning and development. You seek out training opportunities and take initiative to expand your skills and knowledge.

IV: Flexibility and Open-mindedness:

Highlight your flexibility and open-mindedness. You are willing to adapt to new ways of working and are open to feedback and suggestions.

V: Seeking Feedback:

Mention that you actively seek feedback from colleagues and supervisors to ensure you are meeting expectations and making a positive impact.

Example Answer:

"When starting a new job, I first make an effort to research the company culture and observe how things are done. I focus on building relationships with my colleagues and supervisors, as I believe that strong relationships are key to success in any working environment. I also prioritize learning and development, seeking out training opportunities and taking initiative to expand my skills and knowledge.

I approach new situations with flexibility and an open mind, recognizing that there may be different ways of doing things. I actively seek feedback from my colleagues and supervisors to ensure that I am meeting expectations and making a positive impact. Overall, I believe that adaptability and a willingness to learn are key to successfully adapting to a new working environment."

Question 27: Tell me about a situation when you received negative feedback and how you handled it?

"Tell me about a situation when you received negative feedback and how you handled it?" is a behavioral interview question that assesses your ability to accept criticism and use it constructively. Here's how you can approach this question using the STAR method (Situation, Task, Action, Result):

I: Situation:

Describe the context in which you received negative feedback. Explain who gave you the feedback and the nature of the criticism.

II: Task:

Explain the task or goal you were working on when you received the feedback. This could be a specific project, task, or aspect of your job.

III: Action:

Describe the specific actions you took in response to the feedback. Did you ask for clarification? Did you reflect on the feedback and consider how to improve? Did you seek guidance from others?

IV: Result:

Explain the outcome of your actions. Did you use the feedback to make improvements? Did you receive further feedback indicating improvement? Did the situation help you grow professionally?

Example Answer:

"In a previous role, I received negative feedback from a supervisor during a performance review. The feedback was related to my communication skills, specifically my ability to clearly convey complex ideas to clients. My supervisor mentioned that there had been instances where clients had expressed confusion about my explanations.

In response to this feedback, I first thanked my supervisor for the feedback and asked for specific examples to better understand the issue. I then reflected on the feedback and identified areas where I could improve, such as using simpler language and providing more context in my explanations.

I also sought guidance from colleagues who were known for their strong communication skills. I asked them for advice on how to improve my communication with clients and implemented their suggestions.

As a result of this experience, I became more conscious of my communication style and made a conscious effort to simplify my explanations when communicating with clients. Over time, I received positive feedback from clients indicating that they found my explanations clearer and easier to understand. This experience taught me the importance of accepting feedback gracefully and using it as an opportunity for growth."

Question 28: Who's your greatest role model and why do they inspire you?

"Who's your greatest role model and why do they inspire you?" is a question that gives insight into your values, aspirations, and the qualities you admire in others. Here's how you can approach this question:

I: Identify Your Role Model:

Choose a role model who has had a significant impact on your life and whom you admire for their qualities, achievements, or values.

II: Explain Why They Inspire You:

Describe the qualities or achievements of your role model that inspire you. This could include their leadership skills, perseverance, compassion, or dedication to a cause.

III: Relate to Your Own Life:

Explain how your role model's qualities or achievements relate to your own life and aspirations. Mention how they have influenced your goals, values, or actions.

IV: Show Gratitude:

Express gratitude for the positive influence your role model has had on you. Mention how their example has motivated you to become a better person or achieve your goals.

V: Highlight Impact:

Discuss the impact your role model has had on others or society as a whole. Explain why their influence is not only meaningful to you personally but also important on a broader scale.

Example Answer:

"My greatest role model is Nelson Mandela. His leadership, resilience, and dedication to justice and equality inspire me every day. Despite facing immense challenges and adversity, Mandela remained committed to his principles and worked tirelessly to bring about positive change in South Africa.

Mandela's ability to forgive his oppressors and his unwavering belief in the power of reconciliation are qualities that I deeply admire. His commitment to justice and equality serves as a constant reminder to me of the importance of standing up for what is right, even in the face of adversity.

Mandela's impact goes beyond South Africa; he is a global symbol of peace, freedom, and reconciliation. His example inspires me to strive for excellence in everything I do and to work towards a more just and compassionate world."

Question 29: Tell me about a time when you disagreed with your boss?

"Tell me about a time when you disagreed with your boss?" is a behavioral interview question that assesses your ability to handle disagreements professionally and constructively. Here's how you can approach this question using the STAR method (Situation, Task, Action, Result):

I: Situation:

Describe the context in which you disagreed with your boss. Explain the nature of the disagreement and why it occurred.

II: Task:

Explain the task or goal you were working on when the disagreement occurred. This could be a project, decision, or strategy that you and your boss had different opinions about.

III: Action:

Describe the specific actions you took to address the disagreement. Did you express your opinion respectfully? Did you provide evidence or reasoning to support your position? Did you seek compromise or alternative solutions?

IV: Result:

Explain the outcome of the disagreement. Did you reach a resolution with your boss? Did your boss's decision ultimately prove to be the right one? Did the disagreement lead to any positive changes or improvements?

Example Answer:

"In a previous role, I disagreed with my boss about the approach we should take to launch a new product. My boss wanted to launch the product quickly to capitalize on a market opportunity, but I felt that we needed more time to refine the product and ensure a successful launch.

I expressed my opinion to my boss respectfully, highlighting the potential risks of rushing the launch and the benefits of taking more time to refine the product. I also proposed a compromise where we could launch the product in phases, starting with a soft launch to gather feedback and make improvements before a full-scale launch.

My boss listened to my concerns and we had a constructive discussion about the best way forward. Ultimately, we agreed to proceed with a phased launch approach. This decision proved to be successful, as the soft launch allowed us to gather valuable feedback and make improvements that resulted in a successful full-scale launch.

This experience taught me the importance of voicing my opinions respectfully and constructively, even when they differ from those of my superiors. It also taught me the value of compromise and collaboration in finding solutions to disagreements."

Question 30: Tell me about a time you had to deal with a difficult customer?

"Tell me about a time you had to deal with a difficult customer?" is a common behavioral interview question that assesses your customer service skills and ability to handle challenging situations. Here's how you can approach this question using the STAR method (Situation, Task, Action, Result):

I: Situation:

Describe the context of the situation, including the nature of the customer's issue and why it was challenging.

II: Task:

Explain the task or goal you needed to accomplish in dealing with the difficult customer. This could be resolving their issue, calming them down, or finding a solution to their problem.

III: Action:

Describe the specific actions you took to address the difficult customer. Focus on how you remained calm, listened actively, and sought to understand their perspective. Explain any strategies you used to de-escalate the situation and find a resolution.

IV: Result:

Explain the outcome of your actions. Did you successfully resolve the customer's issue? Did the customer leave satisfied? Did you receive any positive feedback or recognition for your handling of the situation?

Example Answer:

"In a previous role, I had to deal with a difficult customer who was upset about a billing error. The customer was frustrated because they had been overcharged for a service and had been trying to resolve the issue for several weeks without success.

I listened carefully to the customer's concerns and empathized with their frustration. I assured them that I would personally look into the issue and find a resolution. I reviewed their account and confirmed that there had been an error in billing. I apologized for the mistake and explained the steps we would take to rectify it.

To resolve the issue, I refunded the customer for the overcharge and offered them a discount on their next service as a gesture of goodwill. I also made sure to follow up with the customer after the issue was resolved to ensure they were satisfied with the outcome.

The customer was appreciative of my efforts and thanked me for resolving the issue promptly and professionally. This experience taught me the importance of patience, empathy, and problem-solving skills in dealing with difficult customers."

Question 31: Tell me about a time when you had to adapt to change?

"Tell me about a time when you had to adapt to change?" is a behavioral interview question that assesses your ability to be flexible and adapt to new situations. Here's how you can approach this question using the STAR method (Situation, Task, Action, Result):

I: Situation:

Describe the situation or context in which you had to adapt to change. Explain what the change was and why it was necessary.

II: Task:

Explain the task or goal you needed to accomplish despite the change. This could be a project, task, or new way of working that required you to adapt.

III: Action:

Describe the specific actions you took to adapt to the change. Focus on how you approached the change with a positive attitude, sought out new information or training, and adjusted your work habits or priorities.

IV: Result:

Explain the outcome of your actions. Did you successfully adapt to the change? How did the change impact your work or the organization? Did you learn anything from the experience?

Example Answer:

"In my previous role, our company implemented a new software system to streamline our workflow. The new system required us to change the way we processed orders and managed inventory, which was a significant change for our team.

To adapt to this change, I first familiarized myself with the new software by attending training sessions and reading documentation. I also sought out guidance from colleagues who were more experienced with the new system.

I then adjusted my work habits to accommodate the new software, making sure to follow the new processes and procedures. I also remained flexible and open-minded, recognizing that there would be a learning curve as we transitioned to the new system.

As a result of my efforts, I was able to adapt to the new software quickly and effectively. I also shared my knowledge and experience with other team members, helping them adapt to the change as well. Overall, this experience taught me the importance of flexibility and adaptability in the workplace."

Question 32: Tell me about a time when you challenged someone's behavior?

"Tell me about a time when you challenged someone's behavior?" is a behavioral interview question that assesses your ability to address interpersonal issues and handle conflicts constructively. Here's how you can approach this question using the STAR method (Situation, Task, Action, Result):

I: Situation:

Describe the situation or context in which you challenged someone's behavior. Explain who the person was and what their behavior was that you found challenging.

II: Task:

Explain the task or goal you needed to accomplish in addressing the behavior. This could be maintaining a positive work environment, upholding company policies, or addressing a specific issue caused by the behavior.

III: Action:

Describe the specific actions you took to challenge the behavior. Focus on how you addressed the behavior directly and professionally, communicated your concerns clearly, and sought a resolution.

IV: Result:

Explain the outcome of your actions. Did the person respond positively to your feedback? Did the behavior change? How did your actions impact the situation or relationship?

Example Answer:

"In a previous role, I worked with a team member who consistently arrived late to meetings and missed deadlines. This behavior not only affected the team's productivity but also created tension within the team.

I decided to address the issue directly with the team member. I scheduled a private meeting with them and explained how their behavior was impacting the team. I used specific examples to illustrate my point and asked for their perspective on the situation.

During the meeting, I discovered that the team member was struggling with personal issues that were affecting their performance at work. I listened empathetically and offered support where I could. I also discussed ways in which we could work together to improve their attendance and performance.

As a result of our conversation, the team member became more aware of the impact of their behavior and made a concerted effort to improve. They began attending meetings on time and meeting deadlines more consistently. Our working relationship also improved, as the team member felt supported and valued.

This experience taught me the importance of addressing behavior issues directly and empathetically. It also reinforced the value of open communication and mutual respect in resolving conflicts."

Question 33: Tell me about a time you helped a co-worker learn a new skill or develop an existing one?

"Tell me about a time you helped a co-worker learn a new skill or develop an existing one?" is a behavioral interview question that assesses your ability to collaborate with colleagues and contribute to their professional development. Here's how you can approach this question using the STAR method (Situation, Task, Action, Result):

I: Situation:

Describe the context in which you helped a co-worker learn a new skill or develop an existing one. Explain why this skill was important and how it related to their role or career development.

II: Task:

Explain the task or goal you needed to accomplish in helping your co-worker develop their skills. This could be improving their performance, preparing them for a new role, or enhancing their professional growth.

III: Action:

Describe the specific actions you took to help your co-worker develop their skills. Focus on how you identified their learning needs, provided guidance and support, and offered constructive feedback.

IV: Result:

Explain the outcome of your actions. Did your co-worker successfully learn the new skill or improve their existing one? How did your support impact their performance or career development?

Example Answer:

"In a previous role, I had a co-worker who was struggling to learn a new software program that was critical to our team's operations. I recognized that mastering this software was important for their professional development and for the team's efficiency.

I offered to help by first assessing their current level of knowledge and identifying areas where they needed improvement. I then created a personalized learning plan for them, which included tutorials, hands-on practice, and regular check-ins to track their progress.

I also provided ongoing support and encouragement, answering any questions they had and offering tips and tricks to help them navigate the software more effectively. I made myself available whenever they needed help and provided constructive feedback to help them improve.

As a result of our efforts, my co-worker was able to master the software and became proficient in using it for our team's operations. Their improved skills not only benefited them personally but also contributed to our team's overall success.

This experience taught me the importance of patience, empathy, and personalized support in helping others develop their skills. It also reinforced the value of teamwork and collaboration in achieving common goals."

Question 34: Tell me about a time when you improved a process?

"Tell me about a time when you improved a process?" is a behavioral interview question that assesses your ability to identify inefficiencies and implement solutions to improve processes. Here's how you can approach this question using the STAR method (Situation, Task, Action, Result):

I: Situation:

Describe the context in which you identified a process that needed improvement. Explain why the current process was inefficient or ineffective.

II: Task:

Explain the task or goal you needed to accomplish in improving the process. This could be streamlining the process, reducing costs, improving quality, or enhancing efficiency.

III: Action:

Describe the specific actions you took to improve the process. Focus on how you analyzed the existing process, identified areas for improvement, and implemented changes. Mention any challenges you faced and how you overcame them.

IV: Result:

Explain the outcome of your actions. Did the process improvement result in cost savings, time savings, or improved quality? How did the change impact the overall workflow or organization?

Example Answer:

"In a previous role, I identified a process in our customer service department that was causing delays in responding to customer inquiries. The process involved manually sorting and assigning incoming emails to different agents based on their expertise, which was time-consuming and prone to errors.

To improve this process, I first conducted a thorough analysis of the current workflow and identified the bottlenecks and inefficiencies. I then proposed a new system that used automated email routing based on keywords and customer profiles, which would ensure that emails were directed to the most appropriate agent automatically.

I worked closely with our IT department to implement the new system and conducted training sessions for the customer service team to ensure they were familiar with the new process. I also monitored the system closely after implementation to identify any issues and make adjustments as needed.

As a result of the process improvement, our response times to customer inquiries improved significantly, leading to higher customer satisfaction ratings. The new system also reduced the workload for our customer service team, allowing them to focus on more complex customer issues.

This experience taught me the importance of continuous improvement and the value of analyzing processes to identify areas for enhancement. It also highlighted the benefits of collaboration across different departments to implement changes successfully."

Question 35: Tell me about a time you missed a deadline?

"Tell me about a time you missed a deadline?" is a behavioral interview question that assesses your accountability, time management skills, and ability to handle setbacks. Here's how you can approach this question using the STAR method (Situation, Task, Action, Result):

I: Situation:

Describe the situation in which you missed a deadline. Explain what the deadline was for and why it was important.

II: Task:

Explain the task or goal you needed to accomplish by the deadline. This could be a project, report, or task that was part of your responsibilities.

III: Action:

Describe the specific actions you took that led to missing the deadline. Be honest about any factors that contributed to missing the deadline, such as unforeseen obstacles, poor time management, or lack of resources.

IV: Result:

Explain the outcome of missing the deadline. How did it impact the project, team, or organization? What did you learn from the experience and how did you rectify the situation?

Example Answer:

"In a previous role, I was responsible for submitting a quarterly report to management by a specific deadline. Despite my best efforts to manage my time effectively, I encountered unexpected delays in gathering the necessary data for the report.

I realized that I had underestimated the time needed to collect and analyze the data, and as a result, I missed the deadline for submitting the report. This delay had a negative impact on the planning and decision-making process for the organization.

To rectify the situation, I immediately informed my manager about the delay and apologized for missing the deadline. I then worked diligently to complete the report as quickly as possible without compromising its quality. I also reassessed my time management strategies and implemented new methods to ensure that I could meet future deadlines more effectively.

This experience taught me the importance of realistic time management and the need to communicate proactively with stakeholders when facing challenges. It also reinforced the value of learning from mistakes and continuously improving my skills."

Question 36: Tell me about a time you demonstrated leadership skills?

"Tell me about a time you demonstrated leadership skills?" is a behavioral interview question that assesses your ability to lead, influence, and motivate others. Here's how you can approach this question using the STAR method (Situation, Task, Action, Result):

I: Situation:

Describe the context in which you demonstrated leadership skills. Explain the project, team, or situation where your leadership was needed.

II: Task:

Explain the task or goal you needed to accomplish as a leader. This could be leading a team to achieve a specific goal, resolving a conflict, or guiding a project to success.

III: Action:

Describe the specific actions you took to demonstrate leadership. Focus on how you communicated effectively, motivated team members, made decisions, and resolved conflicts.

IV: Result:

Explain the outcome of your leadership actions. Did you achieve the goal or resolve the issue? How did your leadership impact the team or organization? What did you learn from the experience?

Example Answer:

"In a previous role, I was tasked with leading a team to implement a new customer relationship management (CRM) system. The project was complex and involved coordinating efforts across multiple departments.

To demonstrate leadership, I first ensured that the team understood the project goals and their roles in achieving them. I held regular meetings to keep everyone informed and motivated, and I encouraged open communication to address any issues or concerns that arose.

I also led by example, working closely with team members to overcome challenges and offering support where needed. When conflicts arose, I facilitated discussions to find solutions that were acceptable to everyone involved.

As a result of my leadership, the project was completed on time and within budget. The new CRM system improved efficiency and customer satisfaction, leading to positive feedback from both internal stakeholders and customers.

This experience taught me the importance of effective communication, collaboration, and problem-solving in leadership. It also reinforced the value of leading by example and supporting team members to achieve common goals."

Question 37: Tell me about a time you made a mistake?

"Tell me about a time you made a mistake?" is a behavioral interview question that assesses your ability to take ownership of your actions, learn from your mistakes, and demonstrate resilience. Here's how you can approach this question using the STAR method (Situation, Task, Action, Result):

I: Situation:

Describe the situation in which you made a mistake. Explain the context and the impact of the mistake.

II: Task:

Explain the task or goal you were working on when you made the mistake. This could be a project, task, or decision that was affected by your error.

III: Action:

Describe the specific actions you took in response to the mistake. Focus on how you took responsibility for the mistake, identified the cause, and took steps to rectify it.

IV: Result:

Explain the outcome of your actions. How did you rectify the mistake? What did you learn from the experience? How did you prevent similar mistakes in the future?

Example Answer:

"In a previous role, I was responsible for managing a project that involved coordinating efforts across multiple teams. During the project, I misinterpreted some important data, which led to a delay in the project timeline.

As soon as I realized my mistake, I immediately informed my supervisor and the teams involved. I took responsibility for the error and worked with the teams to develop a plan to mitigate the delay. This involved reallocating resources and adjusting timelines to ensure that the project could still be completed on schedule.

I also took steps to understand why the mistake occurred and implemented measures to prevent similar errors in the future. This included improving my data analysis skills and seeking input from other team members to verify important information.

As a result of my actions, we were able to complete the project on time, albeit with some adjustments to the timeline. The experience taught me the importance of attention to detail and the value of seeking input from others to verify information. It also reinforced the importance of taking ownership of mistakes and taking proactive steps to rectify them."

Question 38: Tell me about a time when you used your initiative to solve a problem?

"Tell me about a time when you used your initiative to solve a problem?" is a behavioral interview question that assesses your ability to take proactive steps to address challenges. Here's how you can approach this question using the STAR method (Situation, Task, Action, Result):

I: Situation:

Describe the situation or problem that required you to use your initiative. Explain the context and why it was important to find a solution.

II: Task:

Explain the task or goal you needed to accomplish in solving the problem. This could be resolving a work-related issue, improving a process, or addressing a customer concern.

III: Action:

Describe the specific actions you took to solve the problem using your initiative. Focus on how you identified the problem, analyzed the situation, and came up with a solution. Mention any challenges you faced and how you overcame them.

IV: Result:

Explain the outcome of your actions. Did your initiative solve the problem? How did your actions impact the situation or organization? What did you learn from the experience?

Example Answer:

"In a previous role, I noticed that our team was spending a significant amount of time manually updating a report each week. This report was important for tracking our progress on key projects, but the manual process was time-consuming and prone to errors.

To address this issue, I took the initiative to research automated solutions that could streamline the report generation process. After researching several options, I identified a software tool that could automate the report generation and eliminate the need for manual updates.

I presented my findings to the team and proposed implementing the new software tool. I worked with the IT department to set up the software and provided training to the team on how to use it effectively.

As a result of implementing the new software, we were able to significantly reduce the time spent on report generation and eliminate errors. This allowed the team to focus on more strategic tasks and improved our overall efficiency.

This experience taught me the importance of taking initiative and seeking out innovative solutions to solve problems. It also reinforced the value of continuous improvement and finding ways to streamline processes for greater efficiency."

Question 39: Tell me about a time when you saved a company money?

"Tell me about a time when you saved a company money?" is a behavioral interview question that assesses your ability to identify cost-saving opportunities and take action to reduce expenses. Here's how you can approach this question using the STAR method (Situation, Task, Action, Result):

I: Situation:

Describe the situation or context in which you identified an opportunity to save the company money. Explain why it was important to reduce expenses in this area.

II: Task:

Explain the task or goal you needed to accomplish in saving the company money. This could be reducing costs, increasing efficiency, or improving profitability.

III: Action:

Describe the specific actions you took to save the company money. Focus on how you identified the cost-saving opportunity, developed a plan to achieve savings, and implemented the plan. Mention any challenges you faced and how you overcame them.

IV: Result:

Explain the outcome of your actions. How much money did you save the company? How did your actions impact the company's bottom line? What did you learn from the experience?

Example Answer:

"In a previous role, I noticed that our company was spending a significant amount of money on paper and printing supplies. I conducted a thorough analysis of our printing practices and identified several opportunities to reduce costs.

First, I implemented a paperless initiative, encouraging employees to use digital documents instead of printing hard copies. I also negotiated with our printing vendor to secure a lower price for bulk purchases of paper and ink cartridges.

Additionally, I introduced a printing quota system that limited the number of pages each employee could print per month. This helped reduce unnecessary printing and encouraged employees to be more mindful of their printing habits.

As a result of these initiatives, we were able to save the company over $10,000 per year in printing costs. The paperless initiative also had the added benefit of reducing our environmental impact, which aligned with our company's sustainability goals.

This experience taught me the importance of analyzing expenses and seeking out cost-saving opportunities. It also reinforced the value of implementing sustainable practices that benefit both the company and the environment."

Question 40: Tell me about a time when you gave constructive feedback someone?

"Tell me about a time when you gave constructive feedback to someone?" is a behavioral interview question that assesses your ability to provide feedback in a professional and constructive manner. Here's how you can approach this question using the STAR method (Situation, Task, Action, Result):

I: Situation:

Describe the situation or context in which you gave constructive feedback. Explain why it was important to provide feedback in this situation.

II: Task:

Explain the task or goal you needed to accomplish in giving feedback. This could be helping the person improve their performance, correcting a behavior, or fostering their professional development.

III: Action:

Describe the specific actions you took to give constructive feedback. Focus on how you prepared for the feedback conversation, delivered the feedback in a clear and respectful manner, and provided specific examples to support your feedback.

IV: Result:

Explain the outcome of your feedback. How did the person respond to the feedback? Did they take action to improve? How did your feedback impact their performance or behavior?

Example Answer:

"In a previous role, I had a team member who was consistently missing deadlines and not delivering work up to the expected standard. I recognized that providing constructive feedback was essential to help them improve their performance and contribute more effectively to the team.

I scheduled a one-on-one meeting with the team member to discuss their performance. I started the conversation by acknowledging their strengths and the value they brought to the team, but I also expressed my concerns about their missed deadlines and the quality of their work.

I provided specific examples of instances where their performance had fallen short and explained how their actions had impacted the team and the project. I then worked with them to develop a plan to improve their time management skills and quality of work, offering support and guidance along the way.

As a result of our conversation and the feedback provided, the team member was able to improve their performance significantly. They started meeting deadlines consistently and producing work of a higher quality, which had a positive impact on the team's overall performance.

This experience taught me the importance of providing feedback in a constructive and respectful manner. It also reinforced the value of coaching and mentoring to help team members reach their full potential."

Question 41: Tell me about a time when you asked a customer for feedback?

"Tell me about a time when you asked a customer for feedback?" is a behavioral interview question that assesses your customer service skills and your ability to gather and utilize feedback to improve products or services. Here's how you can approach this question using the STAR method (Situation, Task, Action, Result):

I: Situation:

Describe the situation or context in which you asked a customer for feedback. Explain why gathering feedback was important in this situation.

II: Task:

Explain the task or goal you needed to accomplish in asking for feedback. This could be improving customer satisfaction, identifying areas for improvement, or evaluating the effectiveness of a product or service.

III: Action:

Describe the specific actions you took to ask the customer for feedback. Focus on how you approached the customer, what methods you used to gather feedback (e.g., surveys, interviews, feedback forms), and how you ensured the feedback was honest and constructive.

IV: Result:

Explain the outcome of asking for feedback. What did you learn from the feedback? Did you make any changes or improvements based on the feedback? How did the feedback impact the customer's experience or the product/service?

Example Answer:

"In a previous role, I was responsible for managing customer relationships for a software company. We had recently released a new version of our software and wanted to gather feedback from customers to understand their experience and identify areas for improvement.

I reached out to a select group of customers who had been using the new software and asked if they would be willing to participate in a feedback session. I conducted one-on-one interviews with these customers to gather their feedback, asking specific questions about their likes, dislikes, and suggestions for improvement.

I also sent out a survey to a larger group of customers who had used the new software, asking them to rate their experience and provide comments. I made sure to emphasize that their feedback was valuable and would be used to improve the software.

The feedback we received was incredibly valuable. Customers highlighted several areas where the software could be improved, such as adding new features and improving user interface. Based on this feedback, we made several updates to the software that were well-received by customers and improved their overall experience.

This experience taught me the importance of actively seeking feedback from customers and using that feedback to drive improvements. It also reinforced the value of customer relationships and the impact that positive changes can have on customer satisfaction."

Question 42: Tell me about a time when you found a simple solution to a challenging problem?

"Tell me about a time when you found a simple solution to a challenging problem?" is a behavioral interview question that assesses your problem-solving skills and creativity in finding solutions. Here's how you can approach this question using the STAR method (Situation, Task, Action, Result):

I: Situation:

Describe the challenging problem you encountered. Explain the context and why the problem was difficult to solve.

II: Task:

Explain the task or goal you needed to accomplish in solving the problem. This could be overcoming a technical issue, improving a process, or addressing a customer concern.

III: Action:

Describe the specific actions you took to find a simple solution to the challenging problem. Focus on how you analyzed the problem, though creatively about possible solutions, and identified a simple yet effective solution.

IV: Result:

Explain the outcome of your actions. How did your simple solution solve the challenging problem? What impact did it have on the situation or organization? What did you learn from the experience?

Example Answer:

"In a previous role, I was part of a team that was struggling to meet a tight deadline for a project due to a complex issue with our data processing system. The system was generating errors that were causing delays in processing data and could potentially derail the entire project.

After reviewing the system and the errors it was generating, I realized that the root cause of the problem was a simple formatting issue in the data input. Instead of trying to fix the formatting issue within the system, which would have taken a significant amount of time and resources, I proposed a simple workaround.

I suggested that we manually reformat the data before inputting it into the system. This simple solution would bypass the formatting issue and allow us to continue processing data without errors. Despite initial skepticism from some team members, we decided to implement the workaround as a temporary solution.

As a result, we were able to meet the deadline for the project and deliver the final product on time. The simple solution not only solved the immediate problem but also highlighted the importance of thinking creatively and not overlooking simple solutions to complex problems.

This experience taught me that sometimes the simplest solutions can be the most effective, especially when time is of the essence. It also reinforced the value of teamwork and open-mindedness in finding solutions to challenging problems."

Question 43: Tell me about a time when you had to make a quick decision that was going to have a significant impact on the business?

"Tell me about a time when you had to make a quick decision that was going to have a significant impact on the business?" is a behavioral interview question that assesses your ability to make effective decisions under pressure. Here's how you can approach this question using the STAR method (Situation, Task, Action, Result):

I: Situation:

Describe the situation or context in which you had to make a quick decision. Explain the importance of the decision and the potential impact it could have on the business.

II: Task:

Explain the task or goal you needed to accomplish with your decision. This could be addressing a crisis, seizing an opportunity, or resolving a critical issue.

III: Action:

Describe the specific actions you took to make the quick decision. Focus on how you gathered information quickly, evaluated the options available, and made a decision based on the information at hand.

IV: Result:

Explain the outcome of your quick decision. How did your decision impact the business? Did it achieve the desired result? What did you learn from the experience?

Example Answer:

"In a previous role, I was leading a project that was running behind schedule and over budget. We were at a critical juncture where we needed to decide whether to allocate additional resources to the project or to scale back the scope to meet the original timeline and budget.

After reviewing the project status and consulting with key stakeholders, I realized that scaling back the scope was not a viable option as it would compromise the project's objectives. I also recognized that allocating additional resources would have a significant impact on the project budget and timeline.

Given the urgency of the situation, I made the decision to allocate additional resources to the project. I believed that this was the best course of action to ensure the project's success and to minimize any further delays or cost overruns.

As a result of my decision, we were able to complete the project on time and within budget. The additional resources proved to be instrumental in overcoming the challenges we were facing and in delivering a successful outcome for the business.

This experience taught me the importance of making quick and decisive decisions when faced with critical issues. It also reinforced the value of gathering input from key stakeholders and considering all available options before making a decision."

Question 44: Tell me about a time when you had to say no to a customer or client?

"Tell me about a time when you had to say no to a customer or client?" is a behavioral interview question that assesses your ability to manage difficult situations and uphold company policies or standards while maintaining positive customer relationships. Here's how you can approach this question using the STAR method (Situation, Task, Action, Result):

I: Situation:

Describe the situation or context in which you had to say no to a customer or client. Explain why saying no was necessary and the potential impact it could have on the customer relationship or business.

II: Task:

Explain the task or goal you needed to accomplish by saying no. This could be enforcing company policies, protecting company interests, or maintaining ethical standards.

III: Action:

Describe the specific actions you took to say no to the customer or client. Focus on how you communicated the decision clearly and respectfully, listened to their concerns, and offered alternatives or solutions where possible.

IV: Result:

Explain the outcome of saying no. How did the customer or client respond to your decision? Did they understand and accept your explanation? How did your actions impact the customer relationship or business?

Example Answer:

"In a previous role, I was working in customer service for a software company. A customer contacted us requesting a refund for a software product they had purchased, citing that it did not meet their expectations. However, our company policy stated that refunds were only issued for products that were defective or not as described, which was not the case in this situation.

I explained our company policy to the customer and apologized for any inconvenience they experienced. I listened to their concerns and empathized with their situation, but I also made it clear that we were unable to issue a refund based on our policy.

To soften the impact of saying no, I offered alternative solutions, such as providing additional training or support to help them better utilize the software, or offering a discount on future purchases. I ensured that the customer felt heard and valued despite the outcome of the request.

Ultimately, the customer appreciated my transparency and understanding, even though they were disappointed with the decision. They decided to continue using the software and were grateful for the alternative solutions offered.

This experience taught me the importance of maintaining empathy and professionalism when saying no to customers. It also reinforced the value of upholding company policies while still striving to provide excellent customer service."

Question 45: Tell me about a time when you were able to influence change in an organization by only asking questions?

"Tell me about a time when you were able to influence change in an organization by only asking questions?" is a behavioral interview question that assesses your ability to use questioning techniques to drive change and influence others. Here's how you can approach this question using the STAR method (Situation, Task, Action, Result):

I: Situation:

Describe the situation or context in which you sought to influence change in the organization. Explain why change was necessary and the potential impact it could have on the organization.

II: Task:

Explain the task or goal you needed to accomplish by asking questions. This could be understanding the current state of affairs, identifying areas for improvement, or gaining buy-in for a new initiative.

III: Action:

Describe the specific actions you took to influence change through questioning. Focus on the types of questions you asked, how you framed them to encourage critical thinking and discussion, and how you engaged with key stakeholders to drive change.

IV: Result:

Explain the outcome of your questioning and how it influenced change in the organization. What changes were implemented as a result of your questions? How did your questioning impact the organization's culture or operations?

Example Answer:

"In a previous role, I noticed that our team was experiencing frequent delays in project timelines and a lack of collaboration between departments. I believed that improving communication and streamlining processes could address these issues, but I also knew that simply telling people what to do might not be the most effective approach.

Instead, I decided to use questioning techniques to engage with team members and stakeholders. I started by asking open-ended questions to understand their perspectives on the current challenges and what they believed could be done to improve the situation. I also asked probing questions to encourage critical thinking and to challenge assumptions.

Through this process of questioning, I was able to facilitate discussions that led to a deeper understanding of the issues at hand and a shared vision for change. I asked questions that encouraged stakeholders to consider new ideas and approaches, and to take ownership of the change process.

As a result of these questioning techniques, we were able to implement several changes that improved communication and collaboration within the team. This included establishing regular cross-departmental meetings, implementing new project management tools, and providing training on effective communication techniques.

This experience taught me the power of questioning as a tool for influencing change in organizations. It showed me that by asking the right questions and engaging stakeholders in meaningful discussions, you can drive change in a way that is collaborative and sustainable."

Question 46: Tell me about a time when you went above and beyond what was required at work?

"Tell me about a time when you went above and beyond what was required at work?" is a behavioral interview question that assesses your willingness to exceed expectations and your commitment to your work. Here's how you can approach this question using the STAR method (Situation, Task, Action, Result):

I: Situation:

Describe the situation or context in which you went above and beyond at work. Explain why you chose to take on additional responsibilities or put in extra effort.

II: Task:

Explain the task or goal you needed to accomplish by going above and beyond. This could be meeting a tight deadline, exceeding performance targets, or solving a challenging problem.

III: Action:

Describe the specific actions you took to go above and beyond. Focus on how you demonstrated initiative, creativity, or dedication in achieving the task or goal.

IV: Result:

Explain the outcome of your actions. How did going above and beyond benefit the organization or team? Did it lead to recognition, promotion, or other positive outcomes? What did you learn from the experience?

Example Answer:

"In my previous role, we were facing a tight deadline for a project that was critical to the success of the company. The project required extensive data analysis, and the team was struggling to complete the work on time due to the complexity of the data and the volume of work.

Recognizing the importance of the project and the impact it would have on the company, I volunteered to take on additional responsibilities to help the team meet the deadline. I worked long hours, including weekends, to complete the data analysis and prepare the necessary reports.

In addition to my regular duties, I also took the initiative to streamline our data analysis process, which helped us work more efficiently and meet the deadline. I collaborated closely with team members to ensure that we were all on the same page and that everyone was supported throughout the process.

As a result of my efforts, we were able to complete the project on time and deliver high-quality results. My willingness to go above and beyond was recognized by my manager, who commended me for my dedication and commitment to the team.

This experience taught me the importance of stepping up and taking on additional responsibilities when needed. It also reinforced the value of teamwork and collaboration in achieving success in the workplace."

Question 47: Tell me about a time when you took a calculated risk at work?

"Tell me about a time when you took a calculated risk at work?" is a behavioral interview question that assesses your ability to make informed decisions and take calculated risks to achieve positive outcomes. Here's how you can approach this question using the STAR method (Situation, Task, Action, Result):

I: Situation:

Describe the situation or context in which you took a calculated risk at work. Explain why you felt it was necessary to take the risk and the potential impact it could have on the project or organization.

II: Task:

Explain the task or goal you needed to accomplish by taking the calculated risk. This could be achieving a challenging target, exploring a new opportunity, or solving a complex problem.

III: Action:

Describe the specific actions you took to assess the risk and make an informed decision. Focus on how you analyzed the potential outcomes, weighed the pros and cons, and developed a plan to mitigate any potential negative consequences.

IV: Result:

Explain the outcome of your calculated risk. Did it pay off? How did your decision impact the project or organization? What did you learn from the experience?

Example Answer:

"In a previous role, our team was tasked with developing a new product line to expand our market reach. As part of this project, we had the opportunity to explore a new market segment that was relatively untested for our company. While there was potential for significant growth in this market, there was also a considerable risk involved due to the lack of data and market understanding.

After conducting thorough research and market analysis, I felt confident that entering this market segment was a calculated risk worth taking. I presented my findings to the team and proposed a detailed plan outlining the potential benefits and risks, as well as strategies to mitigate those risks.

We decided to move forward with the plan, and I took on a leadership role in executing the strategy. We launched the new product line in the new market segment and closely monitored its performance.

The risk paid off, and the new product line exceeded expectations, generating significant revenue and opening up new opportunities for growth. Our success in this new market segment was largely attributed to the calculated risk we took and the thorough planning and execution that followed.

This experience taught me the importance of taking calculated risks in business and the value of thorough research and planning. It also reinforced the need to be flexible and adapt to changing circumstances to maximize the chances of success."

Question 48: Tell me about a time when you made an unpopular decision?

"Tell me about a time when you made an unpopular decision?" is a behavioral interview question that assesses your ability to make tough decisions and handle the consequences, even when they are not well-received by others. Here's how you can approach this question using the STAR method (Situation, Task, Action, Result):

I: Situation:

Describe the situation or context in which you made an unpopular decision. Explain the background and the reasons why the decision was necessary despite being unpopular.

II: Task:

Explain the task or goal you needed to accomplish by making the unpopular decision. This could be addressing a problem, implementing a change, or upholding company policies.

III: Action:

Describe the specific actions you took to make the unpopular decision. Focus on how you communicated the decision, the rationale behind it, and how you managed any pushback or resistance from others.

IV: Result:

Explain the outcome of your unpopular decision. How did it impact the situation or organization? Did it achieve the desired result? What did you learn from the experience?

Example Answer:

"In a previous role, I was leading a team that was working on a project with a tight deadline. As the deadline approached, it became clear that we were not going to meet the deadline without compromising the quality of our work. After assessing the situation, I made the decision to request an extension to ensure that we could deliver a high-quality product.

This decision was not well-received by some team members who were concerned about the impact on their workload and schedule. However, I believed that it was necessary to prioritize quality over meeting the original deadline.

To communicate the decision, I held a team meeting to explain the reasons behind the request for an extension. I emphasized the importance of delivering a product that met our standards of excellence and explained how the extension would allow us to achieve that.

While some team members were initially unhappy with the decision, they ultimately understood and accepted the rationale behind it. The extension allowed us to deliver a high-quality product that met the expectations of our stakeholders.

This experience taught me the importance of making decisions based on what is best for the overall goals of the project or organization, even if they are not popular with everyone. It also reinforced the value of effective communication in managing difficult decisions."

Question 49: Tell me about a time when you communicated a difficult message to a team or group of people?

"Tell me about a time when you communicated a difficult message to a team or group of people?" is a behavioral interview question that assesses your communication skills, particularly in challenging situations. Here's how you can approach this question using the STAR method (Situation, Task, Action, Result):

I: Situation:

Describe the situation or context in which you had to communicate a difficult message to a team or group of people. Explain why the message was difficult and the potential impact it could have had.

II: Task:

Explain the task or goal you needed to accomplish by communicating the difficult message. This could be delivering bad news, addressing a sensitive issue, or managing a change that might be met with resistance.

III: Action:

Describe the specific actions you took to communicate the difficult message effectively. Focus on how you planned your message, chose the right time and place to deliver it, and used empathy and understanding to connect with the team or group.

IV: Result:

Explain the outcome of your communication. How did the team or group respond to the difficult message? Did they understand and accept it? How did your actions impact the team or group dynamics or the overall situation?

Example Answer:

"In a previous role, I was part of a team that was working on a project that was behind schedule and over budget. It became clear that we needed to make some significant changes to the project plan in order to get back on track, including reallocating resources and extending the timeline.

I was tasked with communicating these changes to the team, which I knew would be difficult news to deliver. I wanted to make sure that the team understood the reasons behind the changes and felt supported throughout the process.

I scheduled a team meeting to communicate the changes, making sure to provide a detailed explanation of why the changes were necessary and how they would benefit the project in the long run. I also took the time to listen to the team's concerns and answer any questions they had.

While the news was initially met with some resistance and disappointment, I made sure to acknowledge their feelings and reassure them that their hard work was appreciated. I also emphasized the importance of working together as a team to overcome the challenges we were facing.

In the end, the team understood and accepted the changes, and we were able to realign our efforts to successfully complete the project. This experience taught me the importance of clear and empathetic communication, especially when delivering difficult messages to a team or group of people."

Question 50: Tell me about a time when you had to work with incomplete data or missing information?

"Tell me about a time when you had to work with incomplete data or missing information?" is a behavioral interview question that assesses your problem-solving skills, adaptability, and ability to make informed decisions in uncertain situations. Here's how you can approach this question using the STAR method (Situation, Task, Action, Result):

I: Situation:

Describe the situation or context in which you had to work with incomplete data or missing information. Explain why the data was incomplete or missing and the potential impact it could have had on your work or project.

II: Task:

Explain the task or goal you needed to accomplish despite the incomplete data or missing information. This could be making a decision, completing a project, or solving a problem.

III: Action:

Describe the specific actions you took to work with incomplete data or missing information. Focus on how you gathered whatever data or information was available, how you analyzed the situation, and how you made decisions or took actions based on the available information.

IV: Result:

Explain the outcome of your actions. How did you manage to complete the task or achieve the goal despite the incomplete data? Did you encounter any challenges along the way? What did you learn from the experience?

Example Answer:

"In a previous role, I was part of a team that was tasked with developing a marketing campaign for a new product launch. We were working with a tight deadline and limited resources, and we encountered a challenge when we realized that we were missing key market research data that was needed to inform our campaign strategy.

Despite this missing information, we knew that we needed to move forward with the campaign planning. I took the initiative to gather whatever data we did have and conducted additional research using available resources, such as industry reports and customer surveys.

I also collaborated closely with other team members to brainstorm creative ideas and develop a flexible campaign strategy that could be adapted once we had more complete data. We focused on creating a campaign that would resonate with our target audience based on the information we did have, while also remaining open to making adjustments as more data became available.

In the end, our campaign was successful, and we received positive feedback from our target audience. While working with incomplete data was challenging, it taught me the importance of adaptability and creativity in problem-solving. It also reinforced the value of collaboration and communication in overcoming challenges in the workplace."

Question 51: Tell me about a time when you created or invented something?

"Tell me about a time when you created or invented something?" is a behavioral interview question that assesses your creativity, innovation, and problem-solving skills. Here's how you can approach this question using the STAR method (Situation, Task, Action, Result):

I: Situation:

Describe the situation or context in which you created or invented something. Explain the background and the problem or need that inspired your creation or invention.

II: Task:

Explain the task or goal you needed to accomplish with your creation or invention. This could be solving a specific problem, improving a process, or creating something new and innovative.

III: Action:

Describe the specific actions you took to create or invent something. Focus on how you identified the problem or need, brainstormed ideas, and developed a plan to bring your creation or invention to life.

IV: Result:

Explain the outcome of your creation or invention. How did it solve the problem or meet the need? What impact did it have on the situation or organization? What did you learn from the experience?

Example Answer:

"In a previous role, I was part of a team that was tasked with finding a solution to improve the efficiency of our inventory management system. We were facing challenges with tracking inventory levels accurately and ensuring that we had the right amount of stock on hand to meet customer demand.

I took the initiative to research new technologies and approaches to inventory management. I identified an opportunity to use RFID (Radio Frequency Identification) technology to track inventory in real-time and automate the replenishment process.

I developed a prototype RFID system and presented it to the team. We worked together to refine the system and integrate it into our inventory management process. The RFID system allowed us to track inventory more accurately and efficiently, reducing the risk of stock outs and overstocking.

As a result of my invention, we were able to improve our inventory management process and reduce costs associated with stock outs and excess inventory. The RFID system also provided valuable data insights that helped us make more informed decisions about our inventory levels and purchasing strategies.

This experience taught me the importance of innovation and creativity in problem-solving. It also reinforced the value of collaboration and teamwork in bringing new ideas to life."

Question 52: Tell me about a time when you left a task unfinished?

"Tell me about a time when you left a task unfinished" is a behavioral interview question that aims to understand your ability to manage tasks, prioritize effectively, and handle situations where you may not have been able to complete a task as planned. Here's how you can approach this question using the STAR method (Situation, Task, Action, Result):

I: Situation:

Describe the situation or context in which you left a task unfinished. Explain why the task was left incomplete and the impact it had on your work or the project.

II: Task:

Explain the task you were working on and why it was important. Describe the goal or objective you were trying to achieve with the task.

III: Action:

Describe the specific actions you took that led to leaving the task unfinished. Be honest about the reasons, whether it was due to unforeseen circumstances, time constraints, or other factors.

IV: Result:

Explain the outcome of leaving the task unfinished. How did it affect the project or your work? What did you learn from the experience and how have you applied this learning in future situations?

Example Answer:

"In a previous role, I was part of a team working on a project with a tight deadline. We were tasked with developing a new product feature that required extensive research and development. I was responsible for conducting the research and presenting my findings to the team.

As the deadline approached, I realized that I was not going to be able to complete the research in time due to the complexity of the task and competing priorities. I made the decision to focus on completing the most critical aspects of the research and present my findings to the team, even though it was not as comprehensive as I had initially planned.

While my presentation provided valuable insights, it was clear that there were gaps in the research that needed to be addressed. The team had to allocate additional resources and extend the deadline to complete the research and development of the feature.

This experience taught me the importance of effective time management and prioritization. I learned that it is essential to communicate early and transparently with team members and stakeholders when facing challenges that may impact project timelines. Since then, I have implemented better strategies for managing my workload and ensuring that tasks are completed on time."

Question 53: Tell me about your proudest professional achievement?

"Tell me about your proudest professional achievement?" is a common interview question that allows you to showcase a significant accomplishment from your career that you are particularly proud of. Here's how you can approach this question using the STAR method (Situation, Task, Action, Result):

I: Situation:

Describe the situation or context in which your achievement took place. Provide background information about the challenge or opportunity you faced.

II: Task:

Explain the task or goal you needed to accomplish. Describe what was expected of you and why the achievement was important in the context of your career or the organization.

III: Action:

Describe the specific actions you took to achieve your goal. Highlight your skills, strengths, and strategies that you used to overcome challenges and accomplish the task.

IV: Result:

Explain the outcome of your achievement. Describe the impact it had on the organization, team, or project. Discuss any recognition or feedback you received as a result of your achievement.

Example Answer:

"One of my proudest professional achievements was leading a cross-functional team to launch a new product that significantly increased our market share. In my previous role as a product manager, I was tasked with developing and launching a new product line to target a specific market segment.

I started by conducting market research and identifying key customer needs and preferences. Based on this research, I developed a comprehensive product strategy and presented it to senior management for approval. Once the strategy was approved, I assembled a cross-functional team consisting of members from marketing, sales, and product development.

I led the team through the entire product development lifecycle, from concept to launch. I coordinated efforts between different departments, ensured that milestones were met, and addressed any issues that arose during the process. I also worked closely with the marketing team to develop a strong branding and marketing strategy for the new product.

The result of our efforts was a successful product launch that exceeded our expectations. The new product received positive feedback from customers and helped us gain a significant market share in the target segment. I was recognized by senior management for my leadership and contributions to the project, which was a proud moment in my career.

This achievement taught me the importance of teamwork, communication, and perseverance in achieving ambitious goals. It also showed me the impact that strategic thinking and effective execution can have on the success of a project."

Question 54: Tell me about a time when you had no choice but to work with limited resources?

"Tell me about a time when you had no choice but to work with limited resources?" is a behavioral interview question that assesses your ability to manage constraints and deliver results in challenging situations. Here's how you can approach this question using the STAR method (Situation, Task, Action, Result):

I: Situation:

Describe the situation or context in which you had to work with limited resources. Explain the nature of the resources that were limited (e.g., budget, time, manpower) and the impact it had on your work or project.

II: Task:

Explain the task or goal you needed to accomplish despite the limited resources. Describe the importance of the task and the challenges you faced due to the constraints.

III: Action:

Describe the specific actions you took to manage the limited resources. Focus on how you prioritized tasks, optimized resource allocation, and found creative solutions to overcome the limitations.

IV: Result:

Explain the outcome of your actions. How did you manage to accomplish the task despite the constraints? What did you learn from the experience?

Example Answer:

"In a previous role, I was part of a team tasked with organizing a large-scale industry conference with a limited budget and tight timeline. We had to secure a venue, coordinate with speakers and vendors, and promote the event to ensure a successful turnout.

Due to budget constraints, we had to be strategic in our decisions and find cost-effective solutions. We decided to host the conference at a local university to save on venue costs and negotiated discounted rates with vendors for catering and audiovisual services.

To promote the event, we leveraged social media and email marketing to reach a wider audience without incurring additional costs. We also reached out to industry influencers and offered them complimentary passes to speak at the conference in exchange for promoting the event to their followers.

Despite the limited resources, we were able to successfully organize and host the conference, which was attended by over 500 industry professionals. The event received positive feedback from attendees and sponsors, and we were able to stay within budget.

This experience taught me the importance of resourcefulness and creativity in managing limited resources. It also showed me the value of effective communication and teamwork in achieving success in challenging situations."

Question 55: Tell me about a time when you used your knowledge or expertise to solve a challenging problem?

"Tell me about a time when you used your knowledge or expertise to solve a challenging problem?" is a behavioral interview question that assesses your problem-solving skills and your ability to apply your knowledge effectively. Here's how you can approach this question using the STAR method (Situation, Task, Action, Result):

I: Situation:

Describe the situation or context in which you faced a challenging problem that required your knowledge or expertise to solve. Explain the nature of the problem and why it was challenging.

II: Task:

Explain the task or goal you needed to accomplish in solving the problem. Describe the importance of solving the problem and the potential impact of not finding a solution.

III: Action:

Describe the specific actions you took to solve the challenging problem using your knowledge or expertise. Focus on how you applied your skills, experience, and understanding of the problem to develop a solution.

IV: Result:

Explain the outcome of your actions. How did your solution solve the problem? What impact did it have on the situation or organization? What did you learn from the experience?

Example Answer:

"In my previous role as a software developer, I encountered a challenging problem where a critical system component was experiencing frequent crashes, leading to downtime and impacting our ability to deliver services to customers. Despite efforts to troubleshoot and resolve the issue, the root cause remained elusive.

Drawing on my knowledge of software architecture and debugging techniques, I decided to take a systematic approach to isolate the problem. I carefully analyzed the logs and error messages to identify patterns and potential triggers for the crashes. I also reviewed the codebase to understand the interactions between different components.

Through this process, I discovered a rare race condition that was causing the crashes under specific circumstances. I proposed a solution that involved adding additional checks and safeguards to prevent the race condition from occurring. I worked closely with the development team to implement the solution and conducted thorough testing to ensure its effectiveness.

As a result of my efforts, we were able to eliminate the crashes and stabilize the system. This significantly reduced downtime and improved our ability to deliver services to customers. The experience taught me the importance of thorough analysis and systematic problem-solving in addressing complex issues."

Question 56: Tell me about a time when you were not going to deliver on a promise you had made?

"Tell me about a time when you were not going to deliver on a promise you had made?" is a behavioral interview question that assesses your integrity, accountability, and how you handle situations when you are unable to fulfill a commitment. Here's how you can approach this question using the STAR method (Situation, Task, Action, Result):

I: Situation:

Describe the situation or context in which you realized that you were not going to deliver on a promise you had made. Explain the nature of the promise and the impact it had on the person or people involved.

II: Task:

Explain the task or commitment you had made and why it was important. Describe the reasons why you were unable to fulfill the promise despite your best efforts.

III: Action:

Describe the specific actions you took to address the situation and communicate with the person or people affected by the unfulfilled promise. Focus on how you took responsibility for the situation and tried to mitigate any negative impact.

IV: Result:

Explain the outcome of your actions. How did you handle the situation? What was the response from the person or people affected? What did you learn from the experience?

Example Answer:

"In a previous role, I was leading a project with a tight deadline, and I had promised my team that we would deliver the project on time. However, as we approached the deadline, it became clear that we were not going to be able to meet it due to unforeseen complications and delays in the project.

Realizing that we were not going to deliver on my promise, I immediately called a meeting with my team to discuss the situation. I explained the challenges we were facing and the reasons why we would not be able to meet the deadline despite our best efforts. I also assured them that I would take full responsibility for the situation and work with them to find a solution.

Together, we brainstormed ideas to mitigate the impact of the delay, such as prioritizing critical tasks and reallocating resources to expedite certain aspects of the project. I also communicated with the stakeholders to update them on the situation and manage their expectations.

While it was a difficult conversation to have, my team appreciated my transparency and willingness to take responsibility for the situation. We worked together to minimize the impact of the delay and delivered the project shortly after the original deadline.

This experience taught me the importance of honesty and communication in leadership. It also reinforced the value of teamwork and collaboration in overcoming challenges and delivering results."

Question 57: Tell me about a time when you did not manage a project properly to get it completed on time?

"Tell me about a time when you did not manage a project properly to get it completed on time?" is a behavioral interview question that aims to assess your project management skills, including your ability to plan, organize, and execute projects effectively. Here's how you can approach this question using the STAR method (Situation, Task, Action, Result):

I: Situation:

Describe the project you were working on and the context in which you were responsible for managing it. Explain the timeline and the importance of completing the project on time.

II: Task:

Explain the task or goal you needed to accomplish with the project and why it was important to complete it on time. Describe any challenges or obstacles you faced in managing the project.

III: Action:

Describe the specific actions you took to manage the project. Focus on how you planned the project, allocated resources, monitored progress, and addressed any issues or delays that arose.

IV: Result:

Explain the outcome of your project management efforts. Did you successfully complete the project on time? If not, what were the reasons for the delay? What did you learn from the experience?

Example Answer:

"In a previous role, I was tasked with managing a project to implement a new software system for our organization. The project had a tight deadline and was critical to improving our operational efficiency. However, despite my best efforts, I did not manage the project properly, and we were not able to complete it on time.

One of the main reasons for the delay was poor initial planning. I underestimated the complexity of the project and did not allocate enough time for certain tasks, such as data migration and user training. As a result, we encountered delays early in the project that set us back significantly.

In addition, I did not effectively communicate with key stakeholders throughout the project. I failed to keep them informed of our progress and any challenges we were facing, which led to misunderstandings and delays in decision-making.

To address these issues, I took a step back and reassessed our project plan. I worked closely with the team to identify critical path tasks and reallocate resources to expedite them. I also improved communication with stakeholders, providing regular updates on our progress and seeking their input on key decisions.

While we were ultimately able to complete the project, it was several weeks behind schedule. This experience taught me the importance of thorough planning, effective communication, and proactive problem-solving in project management. I have since applied these lessons in subsequent projects, resulting in improved outcomes and on-time delivery."

Question 58: Tell me about a time when you made a decision without consulting your manager or supervisor?

"Tell me about a time when you made a decision without consulting your manager or supervisor?" is a behavioral interview question that assesses your decision-making skills, independence, and ability to take initiative. Here's how you can approach this question using the STAR method (Situation, Task, Action, Result):

I: Situation:

Describe the situation or context in which you made a decision without consulting your manager or supervisor. Explain why you felt it was necessary to make the decision independently.

II: Task:

Explain the task or goal you needed to accomplish with the decision and why it was important. Describe any constraints or challenges you faced in making the decision.

III: Action:

Describe the specific actions you took to make the decision without consulting your manager or supervisor. Focus on how you analyzed the situation, weighed the risks and benefits, and made a thoughtful and informed decision.

IV: Result:

Explain the outcome of your decision. Did it achieve the desired result? How did your manager or supervisor react when they found out about the decision? What did you learn from the experience?

Example Answer:

"In a previous role, I was working on a project that was behind schedule and at risk of missing a critical deadline. The project team was struggling to keep up with the workload, and it became clear that we needed to make some changes to our approach to get back on track.

One of the key issues was a lack of communication and coordination between team members. We were using a traditional project management approach that was not well-suited to the fast-paced nature of the project. I felt that we needed to adopt a more agile approach to project management to improve communication and collaboration.

Without consulting my manager, I decided to implement an agile project management framework for the team. I conducted research on agile methodologies and developed a plan to introduce them gradually to the team. I also provided training and support to team members to help them transition to the new approach.

The result of my decision was a significant improvement in team communication and productivity. We were able to meet our deadline and deliver the project successfully. When my manager found out about the decision, they were initially surprised but ultimately pleased with the outcome.

This experience taught me the importance of taking initiative and making decisions independently when necessary. It also showed me the value of being proactive and innovative in finding solutions to complex problems."

Question 59: Tell me about a time you disagreed with a team member?

"Tell me about a time you disagreed with a team member?" is a behavioral interview question that assesses your ability to manage conflict, communicate effectively, and work collaboratively in a team environment. Here's how you can approach this question using the STAR method (Situation, Task, Action, Result):

I: Situation:

Describe the situation or context in which you disagreed with a team member. Explain the nature of the disagreement and why it was important to resolve it.

II: Task:

Explain the task or goal you and your team member were working towards. Describe the impact of the disagreement on the task or goal and the team dynamics.

III: Action:

Describe the specific actions you took to address the disagreement with your team member. Focus on how you communicated your perspective, listened to their perspective, and worked towards a resolution.

IV: Result:

Explain the outcome of the disagreement. Did you and your team member reach a resolution? How did the disagreement affect your relationship with your team member and the overall team dynamics? What did you learn from the experience?

Example Answer:

"In a previous project, I was part of a team tasked with developing a marketing campaign for a new product launch. As we were brainstorming ideas for the campaign, I disagreed with a team member about the direction we should take.

The team member believed that we should focus on traditional marketing channels, such as print and television advertising, to reach our target audience. However, I felt that we should prioritize digital marketing channels, such as social media and online advertising, which I believed would be more cost-effective and reach a larger audience.

Instead of dismissing their idea, I took the time to listen to their perspective and understand their reasoning. I then presented my own perspective, backed up with data and examples of successful digital marketing campaigns in similar industries.

We had a constructive discussion where we both shared our ideas and concerns. In the end, we agreed to incorporate elements of both traditional and digital marketing channels into the campaign to maximize our reach and impact.

The result of our collaboration was a successful marketing campaign that exceeded our expectations. The experience taught me the importance of open communication and collaboration in resolving disagreements within a team. It also showed me the value of considering different perspectives and being open to new ideas."

Question 60: Tell me about a time when a work colleague was not keen to help you?

"Tell me about a time when a work colleague was not keen to help you?" is a behavioral interview question that assesses your ability to manage interpersonal relationships and work collaboratively with others, even in challenging situations. Here's how you can approach this question using the STAR method (Situation, Task, Action, Result):

I: Situation:

Describe the situation or context in which a work colleague was not keen to help you. Explain the nature of the task or request you needed help with and why it was important to seek assistance from your colleague.

II: Task:

Explain the task or goal you needed to accomplish with the help of your colleague. Describe the impact of their reluctance to help on your ability to complete the task or achieve the goal.

III: Action:

Describe the specific actions you took to address the situation and seek help from your colleague. Focus on how you approached your colleague, communicated your needs, and tried to understand their perspective.

IV: Result:

Explain the outcome of your actions. Did you eventually receive help from your colleague? How did their reluctance to help affect your relationship with them and your ability to work together in the future? What did you learn from the experience?

Example Answer:

"In a previous role, I was working on a project that required input from a colleague who was not keen to help me. The project involved developing a new product feature that required collaboration between different teams within the organization.

I approached my colleague and explained the project requirements and why their expertise was crucial to its success. However, they were reluctant to assist me, citing their heavy workload and other priorities.

Instead of being discouraged, I took the time to understand their perspective and the reasons behind their reluctance to help. I offered to assist them with some of their tasks to lighten their workload and showed appreciation for their expertise and contributions to the project.

Eventually, my colleague agreed to help me, and we were able to work together effectively to develop the new product feature. The experience taught me the importance of empathy and understanding in building positive relationships with colleagues. It also showed me the value of patience and persistence in overcoming challenges in a team environment."

Question 61: Tell me about a time when you changed the view of a supervisor or manager?

"Tell me about a time when you changed the view of a supervisor or manager?" is a behavioral interview question that explores your ability to influence others, communicate persuasively, and drive change within an organization.

Here's how you can approach this question using the STAR method (Situation, Task, Action, Result):

I: Situation:

Describe the situation or context in which you were able to change the view of a supervisor or manager. Explain the background of the situation and why it was important to change their perspective.

II: Task:

Explain the task or goal you needed to accomplish and the initial view or opinion of your supervisor or manager. Describe the impact of their view on the task or goal and the need to change it.

III: Action:

Describe the specific actions you took to change the view of your supervisor or manager. Focus on how you presented your arguments or ideas, provided evidence or examples to support your position, and addressed any concerns or objections they may have had.

IV: Result:

Explain the outcome of your actions. How did you successfully change the view of your supervisor or manager? What was their reaction to your efforts? How did this impact the task or goal you were working on and your relationship with your supervisor or manager?

Example Answer:

"In a previous role, I was working on a project that involved implementing a new software system to streamline our internal processes. My supervisor was initially skeptical about the need for the new system, as they believed that our current processes were working fine and that the new system would be too costly and disruptive to implement.

I recognized the importance of gaining their support for the project, so I took the time to understand their concerns and address them proactively. I conducted research to demonstrate the benefits of the new system, such as increased efficiency, cost savings, and improved data accuracy.

I also organized a presentation to showcase the new system's capabilities and how it would address the current challenges we were facing. I invited key stakeholders, including my supervisor, to attend the presentation and ask questions.

After the presentation, my supervisor was impressed by the potential benefits of the new system and how it aligned with our long-term strategic goals. They acknowledged that their initial concerns were unfounded and fully supported the implementation of the new system.

As a result of my efforts, we were able to successfully implement the new software system, which led to significant improvements in our internal processes and overall efficiency. My relationship with my supervisor also improved, as they appreciated my proactive approach and willingness to address their concerns."

Question 62: What would you consider when describing something technical to a non-technical person?

When describing something technical to a non-technical person, it's important to consider the following key points:

I: Simplify the language:

Use simple, jargon-free language that is easy for anyone to understand. Avoid technical terms and acronyms unless you are certain the person is familiar with them.

II: Use analogies and examples:

Use analogies or examples from everyday life to explain complex technical concepts. This can help make the information more relatable and easier to grasp.

III: Focus on the big picture:

Instead of diving into technical details, start by explaining the overall concept or purpose behind the technical topic. This can help the person understand why the information is relevant and how it fits into the broader context.

IV: Use visuals:

Visual aids such as diagrams, charts, or illustrations can be very helpful in explaining technical concepts. They can help convey information more clearly and make it easier for the person to visualize what you are explaining.

V: Check for understanding:

Throughout your explanation, check in with the person to make sure they are following along and ask if they have any questions. Encourage them to ask questions and clarify any points that may be confusing.

VI: Tailor your explanation:

Consider the person's background and knowledge level when explaining technical concepts. Adjust your explanation accordingly to ensure it is appropriate for their level of understanding.

Overall, the key is to communicate clearly, use simple language, and provide relevant examples and analogies to help the person understand the technical information.

Question 63: How do you keep your technical knowledge up to date?

Keeping technical knowledge up to date is crucial in many fields, especially those that are rapidly evolving, such as technology, healthcare, and engineering. Here are some strategies for staying current:

I: Continuous Learning:

Engage in continuous learning through courses, workshops, and seminars. Online Learning offer a wide range of technical courses.

II: Professional Certifications:

Pursue relevant professional certifications in your field. Certifications not only validate your skills but also require you to stay updated with the latest developments.

III: Industry Conferences and Events:

Attend industry conferences, workshops, and networking events. These provide opportunities to learn from experts, discover new technologies, and expand your professional network.

IV: Networking:

Connect with professionals in your field through online forums, social media, and professional associations. Networking can help you stay informed about industry trends and best practices.

V: Read Industry Publications:

Subscribe to industry publications, blogs, and newsletters. Reading articles and blogs written by experts can keep you informed about the latest trends and technologies.

VI: Experiment and Practice:

Hands-on experience is invaluable. Experiment with new technologies, tools, and techniques in a safe environment to gain practical knowledge.

VII: Collaboration:

Collaborate with colleagues on projects or participate in online communities where you can share knowledge and learn from others.

VIII: Feedback and Review:

Seek feedback on your work and review the work of others. This can help you identify areas for improvement and learn new approaches.

IX: Mentorship:

Find a mentor who can provide guidance and advice on your career and technical development.

By staying proactive and using a combination of these strategies, you can keep your technical knowledge up to date and remain competitive in your field.

Question 64: How many golf balls can you fit into a school bus?

The question "How many golf balls can you fit into a school bus?" is a classic example of a type of interview question known as a "brain teaser." These questions are not meant to have a definitive answer but rather to assess a candidate's problem-solving skills, creativity, and ability to think logically under pressure.

To answer this question, you would typically need to make several assumptions and calculations. Here's a general approach you might take:

I: Calculate the volume of the school bus:

Estimate the dimensions of a school bus (length, width, and height) and calculate its volume. For simplicity, you could assume the bus is a rectangular prism.

II: Calculate the volume of a golf ball:

Measure the diameter of a golf ball and use the formula for the volume of a sphere ($4/3 * \pi * r^3$) to calculate its volume.

III: Divide the bus volume by the golf ball volume:

Divide the volume of the school bus by the volume of a golf ball to estimate the maximum number of golf balls that could fit inside the bus.

It's important to note that this question is not about getting the "correct" answer, as the actual number of golf balls that could fit would depend on various factors such as the size of the bus, the size of the golf balls, and how tightly they are packed. Instead, interviewers are interested in how you approach the problem, the assumptions you make, and your ability to think critically and creatively.

Question 65: How do you handle tight deadlines whilst working in a project?

Handling tight deadlines in a project requires effective time management, prioritization, and communication skills. Here are some strategies for managing tight deadlines:

I: Prioritize Tasks:

Identify the most critical tasks that need to be completed to meet the deadline. Focus on completing these tasks first and then move on to less critical tasks.

II: Break Down the Project:

Divide the project into smaller, more manageable tasks. This allows you to focus on completing one task at a time and helps prevent feeling overwhelmed.

III: Set Milestones:

Establish milestones or checkpoints along the way to track your progress. This can help ensure you are on track to meet the deadline and allow you to make adjustments if necessary.

IV: Manage Time Effectively:

Use tools such as calendars, to-do lists, and project management software to schedule your tasks and allocate time for each task. Avoid multitasking, as it can decrease productivity.

V: Communicate Clearly:

Keep your team and stakeholders informed about your progress and any challenges you may be facing. This allows them to provide support or adjust expectations if needed.

VI: Stay Flexible:

Be prepared to adjust your plan if unexpected issues arise. This may involve reprioritizing tasks, reallocating resources, or seeking additional support.

VII: Avoid Perfectionism:

While quality is important, striving for perfection can be time-consuming. Focus on delivering a high-quality outcome within the constraints of the deadline.

VIII: Manage Stress:

Take breaks, practice mindfulness or relaxation techniques, and maintain a healthy work-life balance to prevent burnout.

By applying these strategies, you can effectively manage tight deadlines and deliver successful project outcomes.

Question 66: Tell me about a difficult challenge you had to overcome while working on a project?

"Tell me about a difficult challenge you had to overcome while working on a project?" is a common behavioral interview question that assesses your problem-solving skills, resilience, and ability to handle adversity. When answering this question, it's important to use the STAR method (Situation, Task, Action, and Result) to provide a structured and concise response:

I: Situation:

Briefly describe the project you were working on and the challenge you faced. Provide context to help the interviewer understand the significance of the challenge.

II: Task:

Explain the task or goal you needed to accomplish despite the challenge. Clearly define the objectives and constraints you were working within.

III: Action:

Describe the specific actions you took to address the challenge. Highlight any problem-solving strategies, skills, or resources you utilized. Focus on your contributions and leadership, if applicable.

IV: Result:

Explain the outcome of your actions. Did you successfully overcome the challenge? What impact did your actions have on the project or team? If there were any lessons learned, be sure to mention them.

Example Answer:

"In a recent project, I was tasked with leading a team to implement a new software system for our organization. We were on a tight deadline and faced several challenges, including resistance from team members who were unfamiliar with the new technology.

To address this challenge, I first organized a series of training sessions to familiarize team members with the new software. I also provided one-on-one support to team members who were struggling. Additionally, I worked closely with the software vendor to resolve any technical issues quickly.

As a result of these actions, we were able to successfully implement the new software system on time and within budget. The project was a success, and team members were able to adapt to the new technology smoothly. This experience taught me the importance of effective communication and support when facing challenges in a project."

Question 67: Tell me a time when you worked as part of a team to solve a complex technical task?

"Tell me about a time when you worked as part of a team to solve a complex technical task?" is a behavioral interview question that assesses your teamwork, problem-solving, and communication skills. When answering this question, you can use the STAR method (Situation, Task, Action, Result) to structure your response:

I: Situation:

Briefly describe the project or task you were working on and the complexity of the technical challenge. Provide context to help the interviewer understand the scope and importance of the task.

II: Task:

Explain your role in the team and the specific task or goal you needed to achieve. Describe any constraints or limitations you faced, such as time, resources, or technical expertise.

III: Action:

Describe the specific actions you took as part of the team to solve the complex technical task. Highlight your problem-solving skills, technical expertise, and ability to collaborate with others. Discuss any challenges you encountered and how you overcame them.

IV: Result:

Explain the outcome of your team's efforts. Did you successfully solve the complex technical task? What impact did your solution have on the project or organization? Reflect on what you learned from the experience.

Example Answer:

"In my previous role, I was part of a team tasked with developing a new software application for a client. The client had specific requirements that required us to use complex algorithms and data structures to ensure the application's performance and security.

My role in the team was to design and implement a key component of the application that involved processing large amounts of data in real-time. To solve this complex technical task, I collaborated closely with other team members, including software developers, data scientists, and project managers.

We began by conducting a thorough analysis of the client's requirements and existing systems. We then brainstormed potential solutions and evaluated them based on their feasibility, scalability, and performance. After selecting the best approach, we divided the tasks among team members based on their expertise and began implementation.

Throughout the project, we faced several challenges, such as integrating the new component with existing systems and optimizing performance. However, through effective communication and collaboration, we were able to overcome these challenges and deliver the project on time and within budget.

The result of our efforts was a successful software application that met the client's requirements and exceeded their expectations. This experience taught me the importance of teamwork, communication, and problem-solving in achieving complex technical tasks."

Question 68: How many streetlights are there in this country?

"How many streetlights are there in this country?" is another example of a classic brain teaser interview question. This type of question is not meant to have a specific correct answer but is instead used to assess your problem-solving skills, logical reasoning, and ability to think on your feet. Here's how you might approach this question:

I: Clarify the Scope:

Start by clarifying the scope of the question. Are they asking for an estimate for the entire country, a specific region, or a hypothetical scenario? This will help you narrow down your approach.

II: Make Assumptions:

Since it's impossible to know the exact number of streetlights in a country without specific data, you'll need to make some assumptions. For example, you could assume an average number of streetlights per kilometer of road and then estimate the total length of roads in the country.

III: Calculate an Estimate:

Based on your assumptions, calculate an estimate for the total number of streetlights in the country. You could use data such as the total length of roads, the average distance between streetlights, and the population density to make your estimate.

IV: Explain Your Reasoning:

When presenting your answer, explain the assumptions you made and the reasoning behind your estimate. This will demonstrate your thought process and analytical skills to the interviewer.

It's important to approach these types of questions with a logical and structured mindset, even though there is no definitive answer. The interviewer is more interested in how you approach the problem and your ability to think critically than in the actual number you come up with.

Question 69: Tell me a time when something didn't go to plan. What was the situation and how did you respond?

"Tell me about a time when something didn't go according to plan. What was the situation and how did you respond?" is a behavioral interview question that assesses your ability to adapt to unexpected challenges and problem-solve effectively. When answering this question, you can use the STAR method (Situation, Task, Action, Result) to structure your response:

I: Situation:

Describe the project or task you were working on and the original plan. Explain what happened that deviated from the plan and why it was unexpected or challenging.

II: Task:

Explain the specific task or goal you needed to accomplish despite the unexpected challenge. Describe any constraints or limitations you faced as a result of the change in plans.

III: Action:

Describe the specific actions you took to address the unexpected challenge and get the project back on track. Highlight your problem-solving skills, creativity, and ability to work under pressure.

IV: Result:

Explain the outcome of your actions. Did you successfully overcome the challenge and achieve your goal? What did you learn from the experience, and how did it impact your approach to similar situations in the future?

Example Answer:

"In a previous project, I was leading a team to launch a new product in a tight deadline. Everything was going according to plan until we encountered a major technical issue with the product's software just days before the launch date.

Despite our extensive testing, the issue was unexpected and threatened to delay the launch. To address the challenge, I immediately convened a meeting with the team to assess the situation and develop a plan of action.

We quickly identified the root cause of the issue and divided tasks among team members to address it. Some team members worked on fixing the software issue, while others focused on communicating with stakeholders and developing a contingency plan in case the launch needed to be postponed.

Through our collaborative efforts and round-the-clock work, we were able to resolve the software issue and successfully launch the product on time. This experience taught me the importance of flexibility and teamwork in navigating unexpected challenges and reinforced the value of thorough testing and contingency planning."

Question 70: What can you bring to this role?

"What can you bring to this role?" is a common interview question that allows you to showcase your skills, experiences, and qualities that make you a strong candidate for the position. When answering this question, it's important to tailor your response to match the specific requirements of the role. Here's how you can approach it:

I: Research the Role:

Before the interview, thoroughly research the job description and company to understand the key requirements of the role and the organization's needs.

II: Identify Your Strengths:

Based on your research and self-assessment, identify 2-3 key strengths or qualities that align with the role. These could be skills, experiences, or personal qualities that make you uniquely qualified for the position.

III: Provide Examples:

Support your strengths with specific examples from your past experiences. For each strength, provide a brief example that demonstrates how you have successfully applied that strength in a professional setting.

IV: Relevance to the Role:

Emphasize how your strengths are directly relevant to the role and how they will enable you to contribute to the organization's success. Highlight how your skills and experiences align with the company's goals and values.

V: Value Proposition:

Summarize your answer by highlighting the value you can bring to the role and the organization. Be confident in your abilities and emphasize your enthusiasm for the opportunity.

Example Answer:

"I believe that my strong analytical skills and attention to detail make me a great fit for this role. In my previous role as a data analyst, I was responsible for analyzing large datasets to identify trends and patterns, which helped inform strategic decision-making for the company.

Additionally, my experience working in cross-functional teams has honed my communication and collaboration skills, allowing me to effectively work with colleagues from diverse backgrounds and contribute to a positive team dynamic.

I am also highly motivated and eager to learn, which I believe will enable me to quickly adapt to the challenges of this role and contribute to the continued success of your team."

By providing a tailored and thoughtful response to this question, you can demonstrate your suitability for the role and leave a positive impression on the interviewer.

Question 71: Tell me a time when you worked on a technical project that failed?

"Tell me about a time when you worked on a technical project that failed?" is a behavioral interview question that aims to assess your ability to reflect on past failures, learn from them, and demonstrate resilience. When answering this question, it's important to approach it in a positive and constructive manner. Here's how you can structure your response using the STAR method (Situation, Task, Action, Result):

I: Situation:

Briefly describe the technical project you were involved in that ultimately failed. Provide context about the project, including its objectives, scope, and the team involved.

II: Task:

Explain your role and responsibilities within the project. Describe the specific task or goal you were working to achieve as part of the project.

III: Action:

Describe the actions you took while working on the project. Highlight any challenges or obstacles you encountered and how you attempted to overcome them. Discuss any decisions you made or strategies you implemented to try to make the project successful.

IV: Result:

Explain the outcome of the project and why it ultimately failed. Reflect on what you learned from the experience and how it has influenced your approach to similar projects in the future.

Example Answer:

"In a previous role, I was part of a team tasked with developing a new software application for a client. The project had a tight deadline, and we were under pressure to deliver a high-quality product quickly. Despite our best efforts, the project ultimately failed to meet the client's expectations and was not delivered on time.

As a member of the team, my role was to develop and test specific features of the software. However, as the deadline approached, it became clear that we had underestimated the complexity of the project and overestimated our ability to deliver within the given timeframe.

In response to the challenges we faced, I worked closely with my team members to try to address the issues and salvage the project. We explored alternative solutions, adjusted our timeline, and increased communication with the client to manage expectations.

Despite our efforts, the project was ultimately deemed a failure. However, the experience taught me valuable lessons about project management, teamwork, and communication. I learned the importance of setting realistic expectations, managing scope effectively, and maintaining open lines of communication with stakeholders.

Since then, I have applied these lessons to my work on other projects, ensuring that I approach each new challenge with a clear understanding of the risks and a plan to mitigate them. While the experience was disappointing, it has made me a more resilient and thoughtful professional."

Question 72: Why are manhole covers round?

"Why manhole are covers round?" is a common interview question that assesses a candidate's ability to think logically and creatively. There are several reasons why manhole covers are round:

I: Prevention of Falling In:

A round manhole cover cannot fall into the manhole opening, as it cannot fit through the circular opening. This is not the case with square or rectangular covers, which can fall in if not aligned properly.

II: Ease of Removal and Replacement:

A round shape allows for easy rolling of the cover to move it out of the way. This is particularly important for covers that are very heavy, as it is easier to push and maneuver them in a circular motion.

III: Uniform Distribution of Weight:

The circular shape of a manhole cover allows for an even distribution of weight across its surface. This helps prevent the cover from cracking or breaking under the weight of vehicles or other heavy objects.

IV: Cost-Effectiveness:

Manufacturing round covers is often more cost-effective than manufacturing covers with other shapes. This is because a round shape requires less material and is easier to produce.

V: Historical Precedent:

Round manhole covers have been used for centuries and have become a standard design in many parts of the world. As such, there may be a cultural or historical reason for their continued use.

Overall, the round shape of manhole covers is a practical design choice that has proven to be effective in ensuring safety, ease of use, and cost-efficiency.

Question 73: What would the person who dislikes you the most say about you?

"What would the person who dislikes you the most say about you?" is a challenging interview question that requires you to demonstrate self-awareness, humility, and the ability to reflect on your weaknesses. When answering this question, it's important to be honest and tactful. Here's how you can approach it:

I: Acknowledge the Possibility of Disagreements:

Start by acknowledging that it's natural for people to have different perspectives and that not everyone may see eye-to-eye with you.

II: Focus on Constructive Criticism:

Think about potential criticisms that someone who dislikes you might have, but frame them in a constructive and non-confrontational way.

III: Provide Examples:

If possible, provide examples to support your response. For instance, if the person might say you are too detail-oriented, you could mention a situation where your attention to detail may have caused delays in a project.

IV: Show Growth and Learning:

Explain how you have learned from past criticisms and have taken steps to improve. This demonstrates your ability to accept feedback and grow as a person.

V: Highlight Positive Traits:

Balance your answer by highlighting positive traits that you believe the person might acknowledge, even if they dislike you. This shows that you are aware of your strengths as well as areas for improvement.

Example Answer:

"If someone who dislikes me were to describe me, they might say that I can be overly meticulous or detail-oriented. I've received feedback in the past that my focus on getting every detail right can sometimes slow down a project or make me seem indecisive. While I believe that attention to detail is important, I have learned to balance this with the need to keep projects moving forward and make timely decisions.

However, I also believe that the same person might acknowledge my strong work ethic and dedication to producing high-quality work. Despite any differences we may have, I always strive to deliver results that exceed expectations and am willing to put in the extra effort to achieve this."

By approaching this question with honesty and self-awareness, you can demonstrate to the interviewer that you are open to feedback and committed to personal growth and development.

Question 74: What's the biggest risk you've taken?

"What's the biggest risk you've taken?" is a question that allows you to showcase your ability to take calculated risks and your willingness to step out of your comfort zone. When answering this question, it's important to choose a risk that demonstrates your decision-making process, the potential impact of the risk, and the lessons you learned from the experience. Here's how you can approach it:

I: Choose a Relevant Example:

Select a risk that is relevant to the position you are applying for. Ideally, choose a risk that had a positive outcome or taught you valuable lessons, even if it initially seemed risky.

II: Describe the Situation:

Provide context for the risk by describing the situation or opportunity that presented itself. Explain why you saw it as a risk and what factors you considered before making your decision.

III: Explain Your Decision:

Describe the thought process behind your decision to take the risk. What factors influenced your decision? How did you weigh the potential risks and rewards?

IV: Discuss the Outcome:

Share the outcome of the risk you took. Did it pay off? What were the results? If the risk did not have the desired outcome, discuss what you learned from the experience.

V: Reflect on the Experience:

Reflect on what you learned from taking the risk. Did it help you grow personally or professionally? How has it influenced your approach to risk-taking in the future?

Example Answer:

"One of the biggest risks I've taken was when I decided to leave a stable job to pursue a new career path in a different industry. At the time, I had been working in marketing for several years and had built a successful career, but I felt like I had reached a plateau and was no longer feeling challenged.

I took the risk of leaving my job to pursue a career in digital marketing, a field that was relatively new to me but one that I was passionate about. I knew that making this change would be a significant risk, as I would be starting from scratch in a new industry and would need to learn new skills and build a new network.

However, I believed that the potential rewards outweighed the risks, and I was excited about the opportunity to grow and develop in a new field. Since making the change, I have successfully transitioned into digital marketing and have found it to be incredibly rewarding. I have learned a lot and have grown both personally and professionally as a result of taking this risk."

Question 75: When you encounter issues, what problem solving process do you use?

"When you encounter issues, what problem-solving process do you use?" is a question that aims to understand your approach to problem-solving and how you handle challenges. Your response should demonstrate your analytical skills, creativity, and ability to resolve issues efficiently. Here's how you can approach this question:

I: Define the Problem:

Start by clearly defining the problem or issue you are facing. Make sure you understand the root cause and the impact it has.

II: Gather Information:

Collect relevant data and information related to the problem. This may involve talking to stakeholders, conducting research, or analyzing data.

III: Generate Solutions:

Brainstorm potential solutions to the problem. Consider different approaches and evaluate their feasibility, effectiveness, and potential risks.

IV: Select a Solution:

Choose the most appropriate solution based on your analysis. Consider how each solution aligns with your goals and objectives.

V: Implement the Solution:

Put your chosen solution into action. Develop an action plan, allocate resources, and communicate with stakeholders.

VI: Evaluate the Results:

Monitor the implementation of the solution and evaluate its effectiveness. Determine if the problem has been resolved and if there are any additional steps that need to be taken.

VII: Learn from the Experience:

Reflect on the problem-solving process and identify lessons learned. Consider how you can apply these lessons to future challenges.

Example Answer:

"When I encounter issues, I follow a structured problem-solving process that involves several key steps. First, I define the problem by gathering information and understanding its root cause. I then brainstorm potential solutions, considering their feasibility and potential impact.

Once I have identified a solution, I develop an action plan and implement it, ensuring that all relevant stakeholders are informed. Throughout the process, I regularly communicate with team members and stakeholders to keep them updated on progress and address any concerns.

After implementing the solution, I evaluate the results to determine if the problem has been resolved and if there are any additional steps that need to be taken. Finally, I reflect on the experience to identify lessons learned and apply them to future challenges."

Question 76: Tell me how you'd deal with a client or manager who pushed back on your recommendations?

"When you encounter a client or manager who pushes back on your recommendations, it's important to approach the situation with professionalism, empathy, and a willingness to collaborate. Here's how you can handle this scenario:

I: Listen and Understand:

Begin by listening carefully to the client or manager's concerns. Try to understand their perspective and the reasons behind their pushback. This shows that you value their input and are open to feedback.

II: Clarify and Communicate:

Clarify your recommendations and the rationale behind them. Clearly explain why you believe your recommendations are the best course of action and how they align with the client or manager's goals.

III: Find Common Ground:

Look for areas of agreement and common ground. Emphasize shared objectives and how your recommendations can help achieve them. This can help build rapport and create a more collaborative environment.

IV: Offer Alternatives:

If the client or manager is still hesitant, be prepared to offer alternative solutions. This demonstrates flexibility and a willingness to find a solution that meets their needs.

V: Address Concerns:

Address any specific concerns or objections raised by the client or manager. Provide evidence or examples to support your recommendations and alleviate their concerns.

VI: Seek Compromise:

If necessary, be willing to compromise. Consider adjusting your recommendations or finding a middle ground that addresses the client or manager's concerns while still achieving the desired outcome.

V: Follow Up:

After the discussion, follow up with the client or manager to ensure that any decisions made are implemented effectively. This demonstrates your commitment to addressing their concerns and finding a successful resolution.

Example Answer:

"If a client or manager pushed back on my recommendations, I would first listen carefully to their concerns and try to understand their perspective. I would then clarify my recommendations and the reasoning behind them, emphasizing how they align with their goals and objectives.

If they were still hesitant, I would offer alternative solutions and seek to find common ground. I would address any specific concerns they raised and be willing to compromise if necessary to find a solution that meets their needs.

After the discussion, I would follow up to ensure that any decisions made were implemented effectively and to address any remaining concerns. Overall, I believe that open communication, empathy, and a collaborative approach are key to dealing with pushback from clients or managers."

Question 77: What are your salary expectations?

"When asked about your salary expectations, it's important to approach the question thoughtfully and strategically. Here are some key points to consider:

I: Research:

Before the interview, research the typical salary range for similar positions in your industry and location. Websites like Glassdoor, Payscale, and LinkedIn can provide useful salary data.

II: Consider Your Worth:

Reflect on your skills, experience, and the value you would bring to the role. Consider how your qualifications compare to the job requirements and the market value for similar positions.

III: Be Realistic:

While you want to aim for a salary that reflects your worth, it's also important to be realistic. Consider factors such as the company's budget, the local job market, and the overall economic climate.

IV: Provide a Range:

When asked about your salary expectations, it's often best to provide a range rather than a specific number. This allows for flexibility and negotiation.

V: Factor in Benefits:

Remember to consider benefits such as healthcare, retirement contributions, vacation time, and other perks when considering your salary expectations.

VI: Tailor Your Response:

Your salary expectations may vary depending on the specifics of the job, such as the responsibilities, the company's size and reputation, and the opportunity for growth and advancement.

Example Answer:

"Based on my research and the responsibilities of the role, I would expect a salary in the range of $X to $Y per year. However, I'm open to discussing the details, including benefits and opportunities for advancement, to ensure that it's a mutually beneficial arrangement."

By approaching the question thoughtfully and providing a well-reasoned response, you can demonstrate your professionalism and set the stage for a constructive salary negotiation process."

Question 78: Describe your work ethic?

When asked to describe your work ethic, the interviewer is seeking insight into your approach to work, your values, and how you handle professional responsibilities. Here's how you can approach this question:

I: Define Your Work Ethic:

Start by defining what work ethic means to you. For example, you might say that you believe in being diligent, reliable, and committed to producing high-quality work.

II: Provide Examples:

Illustrate your work ethic with examples from your work experience. Discuss times when you went above and beyond, worked under pressure, or demonstrated a strong commitment to achieving results.

III: Highlight Your Values:

Explain the values that underpin your work ethic. This might include integrity, accountability, professionalism, or a focus on continuous improvement.

IV: Discuss Your Approach to Challenges:

Describe how you approach challenges and setbacks in the workplace. Talk about your problem-solving skills, resilience, and ability to stay motivated in difficult situations.

V: Connect Your Work Ethic to the Job:

Tailor your response to align with the requirements of the job. For example, if the job requires teamwork, you might discuss your collaborative approach to work.

Example Answer:

"I would describe my work ethic as diligent and results-driven. I believe in putting in the effort required to achieve my goals and consistently delivering high-quality work. For example, in my previous role, I was tasked with leading a project with a tight deadline. Despite the challenges, I organized my team effectively, delegated tasks based on each team member's strengths, and ensured that we met the deadline without compromising on quality.

Integrity is also important to me. I believe in being honest and transparent in all my dealings, whether with colleagues, clients, or stakeholders. This commitment to integrity has earned me the trust and respect of my peers and has helped me build strong working relationships.

I also value continuous learning and improvement. I actively seek out opportunities to expand my skills and knowledge, whether through formal training programs or informal learning experiences. This mindset has helped me adapt to new challenges and stay ahead in a rapidly changing work environment.

Overall, my work ethic is driven by a desire to achieve excellence in everything I do and to make a positive impact in the workplace."

Question 79: How do you prioritize your work?

When asked how you prioritize your work, the interviewer is trying to assess your organizational skills, time management abilities, and how you handle multiple tasks or projects. Here's how you can approach this question:

I: Explain Your Process:

Describe your approach to prioritizing work. This might include creating to-do lists, using a prioritization framework (such as the Eisenhower Matrix or ABC method), or relying on deadlines and importance to guide your decisions.

II: Consider Urgency and Importance:

Explain how you differentiate between urgent and important tasks. Share how you ensure that urgent tasks are addressed promptly while also focusing on tasks that are important for long-term goals.

III: Adaptability:

Highlight your ability to adapt your priorities based on changing circumstances. Discuss how you handle unexpected tasks or shifting priorities without sacrificing the quality of your work.

IV: Time Management Techniques:

Mention any time management techniques or tools you use to stay organized and on track. This could include setting deadlines, using calendars or task management apps, or batching similar tasks together.

V: Communication:

Explain how you communicate your priorities to colleagues or supervisors. Discuss how you collaborate with others to ensure alignment and avoid conflicts in priorities.

Example Answer:

"I prioritize my work by first assessing the urgency and importance of each task. I use a combination of deadlines and the impact on our team's goals to determine the priority level. For example, if a task is both urgent and directly contributes to our team's overall objectives, it will be a top priority.

I also rely on to-do lists and digital tools like Trello to keep track of tasks and deadlines. I break down larger projects into smaller, more manageable tasks and assign deadlines to each one. This helps me stay organized and ensures that I'm making progress on multiple fronts.

Additionally, I regularly communicate with my team to understand their priorities and adjust my own as needed. This collaborative approach helps us stay aligned and ensures that we're working towards our common goals.

In situations where priorities change suddenly, I remain flexible and adapt quickly. I reassess my to-do list and adjust my schedule as needed to accommodate new tasks or changes in priorities. This adaptability has helped me manage multiple projects successfully and deliver high-quality work on time."

Question 80: What will you do in the first 30 days of starting work here?

When asked what you would do in the first 30 days of starting a new job, the interviewer is looking to understand your approach to onboarding and how you would ramp up quickly in a new role. Here's how you can approach this question:

I: Understand the Job and Company:

Start by familiarizing yourself with the job description and the company's mission, values, and culture. This will help you understand what is expected of you and how you can contribute effectively.

II: Build Relationships:

Identify key stakeholders, including team members, managers, and cross-functional partners, and schedule meetings to introduce yourself. Building strong relationships early on is crucial for collaboration and success in your new role.

III: Learn the Tools and Processes:

Familiarize yourself with the tools, software, and processes used in the company. This may include project management tools, communication platforms, and any specific software or systems relevant to your role.

IV: Set Clear Goals:

Work with your manager to set clear, achievable goals for your first 30 days. These goals should align with your role and the company's objectives and should be measurable to track your progress.

V: Seek Feedback:

Actively seek feedback from your manager and colleagues to understand how you can improve and adapt to your new role. Use this feedback to make adjustments and refine your approach.

VI: Contribute Where Possible:

Look for opportunities to contribute and add value from day one. This could involve taking on small projects, offering insights based on your previous experience, or assisting colleagues with their work.

VII: Reflect and Adjust:

Regularly reflect on your progress and adjust your approach as needed. Use this time to identify any gaps in your knowledge or skills and take proactive steps to address them.

Example Answer:

"In the first 30 days of starting work here, my focus would be on learning, building relationships, and contributing to the team. I would start by immersing myself in the company culture and values, getting to know my team members and key stakeholders, and understanding the expectations for my role.

I would also familiarize myself with the tools and processes used in the company, seeking training or guidance where needed. Setting clear goals with my manager would be a priority, ensuring that they align with the company's objectives and are measurable.

I would seek feedback regularly to ensure that I am on track and making a positive impact. Additionally, I would look for opportunities to contribute where possible, whether by taking on small projects or assisting colleagues.

Overall, my goal for the first 30 days would be to establish myself as a valuable member of the team and set a strong foundation for success in my new role."

Question 81: What motivates you?

"When asked about your motivations, the interviewer is trying to understand what drives you professionally and what keeps you engaged and productive. Here's how you can approach this question:

I: Personal Growth:

Highlight your desire for personal and professional growth. Talk about how you are motivated by the opportunity to learn new skills, take on new challenges, and develop your expertise.

II: Achievement:

Discuss how you are driven by a sense of achievement and accomplishment. Share examples of goals you have set and achieved in the past, and how these experiences have motivated you to continue pushing yourself.

III: Making an Impact:

Explain how you are motivated by the opportunity to make a positive impact. Discuss how you are driven by a desire to contribute to something meaningful and to see the results of your work making a difference.

IV: Recognition:

Mention how you are motivated by recognition and feedback. Discuss how positive feedback and acknowledgment of your contributions motivate you to continue performing at a high level.

V: Teamwork and Collaboration:

If applicable, talk about how you are motivated by teamwork and collaboration. Share how you enjoy working with others towards a common goal and how the support of a team motivates you to do your best work.

VI: Job Satisfaction:

Lastly, mention how job satisfaction and a sense of fulfillment motivate you. Discuss how you are motivated by enjoying your work and feeling fulfilled by the work you do.

Example Answer:

"What motivates me is the opportunity for personal growth and development. I thrive in environments where I can learn new skills, take on new challenges, and continually improve. For example, in my previous role, I took the initiative to learn a new programming language, which not only helped me in my current role but also opened up new opportunities for me within the company.

I am also motivated by the opportunity to make an impact. I find satisfaction in knowing that my work is contributing to the success of the team and the organization as a whole. Whether it's coming up with a creative solution to a problem or collaborating with colleagues to achieve a shared goal, I am driven by the idea that my efforts are making a difference.

Additionally, I am motivated by recognition and feedback. Knowing that my contributions are valued and appreciated motivates me to continue performing at a high level. I believe that a positive work environment, where employees feel valued and supported, is crucial for achieving success."

Question 82: How would you handle a challenging client?

When faced with a challenging client, it's important to approach the situation with professionalism, empathy, and a focus on finding a mutually beneficial resolution. Here's how you can handle this question:

I: Listen and Understand:

Start by listening carefully to the client's concerns. Allow them to express their frustrations and concerns fully without interruption. This demonstrates empathy and shows that you are taking their concerns seriously.

II: Stay Calm and Professional:

Maintain a calm and professional demeanor, even if the client becomes confrontational or agitated. Avoid responding emotionally and instead focus on finding a solution to the problem.

III: Acknowledge Their Concerns:

Acknowledge the client's concerns and validate their feelings. Let them know that you understand why they are upset and that you are committed to finding a resolution.

IV: Propose Solutions:

Once you have a clear understanding of the client's concerns, propose practical solutions to address them. Be prepared to negotiate and find a compromise that meets both the client's needs and your company's policies.

V: Set Boundaries:

While it's important to be empathetic, it's also important to set boundaries and maintain professional standards. If the client's behavior becomes abusive or unreasonable, calmly but firmly assert your boundaries and escalate the issue to a supervisor if necessary.

VI: Follow Up:

After the situation has been resolved, follow up with the client to ensure that they are satisfied with the outcome. This demonstrates your commitment to customer service and can help rebuild trust and rapport.

Example Answer:

"If I were faced with a challenging client, my first step would be to listen carefully to their concerns and validate their feelings. I would let them know that I understand why they are upset and that I am committed to finding a resolution. I would then propose practical solutions to address their concerns, taking into account both their needs and our company's policies.

Throughout the process, I would maintain a calm and professional demeanor, even if the client becomes confrontational. I would set boundaries and assert them firmly if the client's behavior becomes abusive or unreasonable. After the situation has been resolved, I would follow up with the client to ensure that they are satisfied with the outcome and to demonstrate our commitment to their satisfaction."

Question 83: What's the difference between leadership and management?

"Leadership and management are often used interchangeably, but they refer to different aspects of guiding a team or organization. Here's a breakdown of the key differences between the two:

I: Vision vs. Implementation:

Leadership is more about setting a vision and inspiring others to follow it. Leaders focus on the big picture, setting goals, and charting a course for the future. On the other hand, management is about implementing the vision set by leaders. Managers focus on organizing, planning, and controlling to achieve the established goals.

II: Inspiration vs. Direction:

Leaders inspire and motivate their teams to achieve greatness. They lead by example, embodying the values and principles they want their teams to follow. Managers, on the other hand, provide direction and guidance to their teams. They ensure that tasks are completed efficiently and effectively.

III: Focus on People vs. Focus on Tasks:

Leadership is primarily about people. Leaders focus on building relationships, developing talent, and empowering others to succeed. They prioritize the growth and well-being of their team members. Management, on the other hand, is more task-oriented. Managers focus on organizing work, assigning tasks, and ensuring that deadlines are met.

IV: Long-Term vs. Short-Term Perspective:

Leaders have a long-term perspective, focusing on the future and the organization's long-term success. They anticipate change, innovate, and adapt to new challenges. Managers, on the other hand, have a more short-term perspective, focusing on day-to-day operations and immediate goals.

V: Risk-Taking vs. Risk Management:

Leaders are often willing to take risks and embrace uncertainty in pursuit of their vision. They are comfortable stepping out of their comfort zone and exploring new opportunities. Managers, on the other hand, are more focused on managing risks and ensuring that projects are completed successfully and within budget.

In summary, while leadership and management are closely related, they are distinct concepts. Leadership is about setting a vision, inspiring others, and focusing on the big picture, while management is about implementing the vision, organizing work, and ensuring that tasks are completed efficiently."

Question 84: What's your leadership style?

When discussing your leadership style, it's important to consider the context of the role and the organization. Here are some common leadership styles and how you might elaborate on them:

I: Autocratic:

In an autocratic leadership style, the leader makes decisions without consulting team members. This style can be effective in situations where quick decisions are needed or when the leader has a high level of expertise.

II: Democratic:

A democratic leadership style involves involving team members in the decision-making process. This can lead to higher levels of employee engagement and buy-in, as team members feel their opinions are valued.

III: Laissez-Faire:

In a laissez-faire leadership style, the leader takes a hands-off approach and allows team members to make decisions on their own. This style can be effective when team members are highly skilled and motivated.

IV: Transformational:

Transformational leaders inspire and motivate their teams to achieve greatness. They often have a clear vision and are able to communicate it effectively, inspiring others to follow their lead.

V: Transactional:

Transactional leaders focus on setting clear goals and expectations for their teams. They use rewards and punishments to motivate team members to achieve these goals.

VI: Servant:

Servant leaders prioritize the needs of their team members above their own. They focus on serving their team and helping them to grow and develop.

VII: Charismatic:

Charismatic leaders have a strong personality and are able to inspire and motivate others through their charisma and enthusiasm.

When discussing your leadership style in an interview, it's important to highlight the positive aspects of your approach and how it has led to successful outcomes in the past. You should also be prepared to discuss any challenges you have faced and how you have adapted your style to overcome them.

Question 85: How would you motivate a team?

Motivating a team requires a combination of understanding individual motivations, creating a positive work environment, and providing meaningful incentives. Here's how you can elaborate on motivating a team:

I: Understanding Individual Motivations:

Get to know your team members on a personal level to understand what motivates each of them. Some may be motivated by recognition, while others may be motivated by challenging work or opportunities for growth.

II: Setting Clear Goals:

Clearly communicate the team's goals and how each team member contributes to those goals. This helps create a sense of purpose and direction, motivating team members to work towards a common objective.

III: Providing Support and Resources:

Ensure that your team has the resources they need to succeed, whether it's training, tools, or support from other team members. This shows that you are invested in their success, which can be a powerful motivator.

IV: Offering Recognition and Rewards:

Recognize and reward team members for their achievements and contributions. This can be as simple as a verbal acknowledgment or as formal as a bonus or promotion. Recognition and rewards help reinforce positive behavior and motivate team members to continue performing at a high level.

V: Encouraging Collaboration and Teamwork:

Foster a culture of collaboration and teamwork where team members support and encourage each other. This creates a sense of camaraderie and belonging, which can be motivating.

VI: Providing Opportunities for Growth:

Offer opportunities for team members to grow and develop their skills. This could include training programs, mentoring, or opportunities to take on new responsibilities. Growth opportunities can be a powerful motivator for many team members.

VII: Leading by Example:

As a leader, your behavior sets the tone for the team. Demonstrate the qualities and behaviors you want to see in your team, such as hard work, dedication, and positivity. Your example can inspire and motivate others to do the same.

When discussing how you would motivate a team in an interview, be sure to provide specific examples from your past experience and explain the impact your approach had on team performance and morale.

Q86. What was the last podcast you listened to or book that you read?

When discussing the last podcast you listened to or book you read in an interview, it's important to choose something relevant to the job or that demonstrates your interests and values. Here's how you can elaborate on your answer:

I: Podcast:

If you listened to a podcast, explain why you chose that particular episode or series. Discuss any insights or ideas you found interesting and how they relate to your professional or personal life. For example, if you listened to a podcast about leadership, you could talk about how the episode's advice on communication resonated with you and how you plan to apply it in your own leadership style.

II: Book:

If you read a book, summarize the main themes and ideas. Discuss how the book impacted your thinking or perspective. For example, if you read a book on time management, you could talk about how the author's tips for prioritizing tasks have helped you become more organized and efficient in your work.

III: Relevance to the Job:

Whenever possible, try to tie your podcast or book choice back to the job you're interviewing for. For example, if you're interviewing for a marketing role, you could discuss a podcast episode that provided insights into the latest trends in digital marketing.

IV: Personal Growth:

Highlight how the podcast or book contributed to your personal growth and development. This could include gaining new knowledge or skills, changing your perspective on a certain issue, or inspiring you to take action in some way.

V: Curiosity and Learning:

Emphasize your curiosity and passion for learning by discussing how you actively seek out new ideas and perspectives through podcasts and books. This demonstrates to the interviewer that you are proactive about your own development.

Example Answer:

"The last podcast I listened to was an episode on the future of work. It discussed how remote work and digital technologies are reshaping the way we work and collaborate. I found the episode fascinating because it touched on many of the trends I've been following in my own work, such as the rise of virtual teams and the importance of digital skills. It reinforced my belief that continuous learning and adaptation are key to staying relevant in today's fast-paced work environment. I plan to apply some of the insights from the podcast to my own approach to work, particularly in terms of embracing new technologies and finding innovative ways to collaborate with colleagues."

Question 87: What are the most important qualities needed to work in a team?

Working in a team requires a specific set of qualities to ensure effective collaboration and achieve common goals. Here are some important qualities needed to work in a team:

I: Communication:

Effective communication is essential for team members to understand each other's perspectives, share ideas, and coordinate tasks. Good communicators are able to express their thoughts clearly and listen actively to others.

II: Collaboration:

Teamwork requires a willingness to collaborate with others, share responsibilities, and work towards common objectives. Collaborative team members are able to build on each other's strengths and support each other's growth.

II: Reliability:

Reliable team members can be depended on to complete their tasks on time and meet deadlines. They take their responsibilities seriously and follow through on their commitments.

III: Adaptability:

In a dynamic work environment, team members need to be adaptable and flexible. They should be able to adjust to changing circumstances, take on new roles when needed, and respond positively to feedback.

IV: Problem-solving:

Strong problem-solving skills are essential for teams to overcome challenges and find innovative solutions. Team members should be able to analyze problems, identify root causes, and develop effective strategies to address them.

V: Respectfulness:

Respectful team members value the opinions and contributions of others. They treat their colleagues with courtesy and professionalism, creating a positive and inclusive team environment.

VI: Leadership:

While leadership is often associated with formal roles, such as team leaders or managers, all team members can demonstrate leadership qualities. This includes taking initiative, motivating others, and providing guidance when needed.

VII: Conflict Resolution:

Conflicts are inevitable in any team setting, but how they are resolved can determine the team's success. Team members should be able to manage conflicts constructively, listen to different viewpoints, and find mutually acceptable solutions.

VIII: Emotional Intelligence:

Emotional intelligence involves being aware of your own emotions and those of others, and using this awareness to manage your behavior and relationships effectively. Team members with high emotional intelligence are better able to navigate interpersonal dynamics and build strong relationships with their colleagues.

IX: Commitment:

Finally, team members should be committed to the team's goals and objectives. They should be willing to put in the effort and time required to achieve success, and be supportive of their team members in the process.

When discussing the most important qualities needed to work in a team in an interview, you can emphasize how you have demonstrated these qualities in your past experiences and how you would contribute to a positive and productive team environment in the future.

Question 88: Describe a time when you had to work at pace?

"Describe a time when you had to work at pace" is a question that aims to assess your ability to handle a fast-paced work environment and manage multiple tasks efficiently. When answering this question, follow the STAR method (Situation, Task, Action, Result) to provide a structured and detailed response:

I: Situation:

Start by briefly setting the scene for the interviewer. Describe the context of the situation, including the company you were working for, your role, and the project or task you were working on.

II: Task:

Explain the task or goal you needed to accomplish and the deadlines or time constraints you were facing. Make sure to emphasize the importance of working quickly and efficiently to meet these deadlines.

III: Action:

Describe the specific actions you took to work at pace. Highlight any strategies or techniques you used to manage your time effectively, prioritize tasks, and stay focused under pressure. Mention any collaboration or delegation efforts if applicable.

IV: Result:

Finally, explain the outcome of your efforts. Did you successfully meet the deadlines or achieve the desired results? If so, how did your ability to work at pace contribute to this success? If there were any challenges or setbacks along the way, discuss how you overcame them and what you learned from the experience.

Example Answer:

"In my previous role as a project manager, I was tasked with leading a team to launch a new product within a tight deadline. We had just six weeks to complete the project, from initial concept to final launch. To work at pace, I immediately set up a project timeline with clear milestones and deadlines for each phase of the project.

I also conducted daily stand-up meetings with the team to ensure everyone was on track and to address any issues or roadblocks quickly. I prioritized tasks based on their importance and urgency, and I was proactive in identifying potential risks and developing mitigation plans.

Despite the tight deadline, we were able to successfully launch the product on time and within budget. Our ability to work at pace was crucial to this success, and it demonstrated my strong organizational skills and ability to perform under pressure."

Question 89: Tell me about a time when you had to overcome a disagreement?

"Tell me about a time when you had to overcome a disagreement" is a behavioral interview question that assesses your conflict resolution skills and ability to work collaboratively with others. When responding to this question, use the STAR method (Situation, Task, Action, Result) to provide a structured and comprehensive answer:

I: Situation:

Describe the context of the disagreement. Provide details about the project, team, and individuals involved. Explain the nature of the disagreement and why it was important to resolve it.

II: Task:

Explain the goal or objective that was being hindered by the disagreement. Highlight the importance of finding a resolution and the impact it was having on the project or team dynamics.

III: Action:

Describe the specific steps you took to address and resolve the disagreement. Emphasize your communication and negotiation skills, as well as your ability to listen actively and empathize with the other party's perspective. Mention any compromises or concessions you made to reach a resolution.

IV: Result:

Explain the outcome of your efforts to overcome the disagreement. Did you reach a mutual agreement or compromise? How did this resolution impact the project or team dynamics? Reflect on what you learned from the experience and how you would approach similar situations in the future.

Example Answer:

"In a previous role, my team was working on a project that required us to collaborate closely with another department. However, there was a disagreement between my team and the other department regarding the scope of work and allocation of resources. The disagreement was causing delays in the project and impacting team morale.

To overcome this disagreement, I first scheduled a meeting with the other department to discuss our concerns openly and transparently. I listened carefully to their perspective and asked probing questions to understand their underlying concerns. I then proposed a compromise that involved reallocating resources and adjusting the scope of work to better align with both teams' needs.

After some negotiation and further discussion, we were able to reach a mutual agreement that satisfied both teams. As a result, the project was able to move forward smoothly, and team morale improved. This experience taught me the importance of open communication, empathy, and collaboration in overcoming disagreements and achieving common goals."

Question 90: Tell me about a time when you had a difficult interaction with a customer?

"Tell me about a time when you had a difficult interaction with a customer" is a common behavioral interview question that assesses your customer service skills, problem-solving abilities, and ability to handle challenging situations. When answering this question, use the STAR method (Situation, Task, Action, Result) to provide a structured and detailed response:

I: Situation:

Describe the context of the difficult interaction. Provide details about the customer, the nature of the problem or complaint, and any other relevant background information.

II: Task:

Explain the goal or objective of the interaction. For example, the goal may have been to resolve the customer's issue, address their concerns, and ensure their satisfaction.

III: Action:

Describe the specific actions you took to address the difficult interaction. Highlight your communication skills, empathy, and ability to remain calm under pressure. Explain how you listened to the customer's concerns, asked clarifying questions, and worked to find a solution.

IV: Result:

Explain the outcome of the interaction. Did you successfully resolve the customer's issue and satisfy their needs? How did the customer respond to your efforts? Reflect on what you learned from the experience and how you would approach similar situations in the future.

Example Answer:

"In my previous role as a customer service representative, I had a difficult interaction with a customer who was unhappy with the quality of a product they had purchased. The customer was frustrated and angry, and they expressed their dissatisfaction in a very confrontational manner.

To address the situation, I first listened to the customer's concerns without interrupting, allowing them to fully express their frustration. I then empathized with their situation and apologized for any inconvenience they had experienced. I asked clarifying questions to better understand the issue and assured the customer that I would do everything in my power to resolve it.

After investigating the issue further, I discovered that there had been a mistake in the product packaging, which had led to the quality issue. I offered the customer a refund or a replacement product, whichever they preferred. I also took steps to prevent similar issues from occurring in the future by implementing a more thorough quality control process.

In the end, the customer was satisfied with the resolution and thanked me for my help. This experience taught me the importance of active listening, empathy, and problem-solving skills in handling difficult customer interactions."

Question 91: Tell me about a time when you helped develop the career of a co-worker?

"Tell me about a time when you helped develop the career of a co-worker" is a behavioral interview question that assesses your ability to mentor, coach, and support the professional growth of your colleagues. When answering this question, use the STAR method (Situation, Task, Action, Result) to provide a structured and detailed response:

I: Situation:

Describe the context of the situation. Provide details about your co-worker, their career goals, and the challenges they were facing in their professional development.

II: Task:

Explain the goal or objective of helping develop your co-worker's career. For example, the goal may have been to help them acquire new skills, advance to a higher position, or overcome a specific challenge.

III: Action:

Describe the specific actions you took to support your co-worker's career development. Highlight your mentoring or coaching skills, as well as your ability to provide constructive feedback and guidance. Explain how you identified their strengths and areas for improvement, and how you tailored your approach to their individual needs.

IV: Result:

Explain the outcome of your efforts to develop your co-worker's career. Did they acquire new skills, advance in their career, or overcome the challenges they were facing? How did your support contribute to their professional growth? Reflect on what you learned from the experience and how you would approach similar situations in the future.

Example Answer:

"In my previous role, I had a co-worker who expressed an interest in advancing to a higher position within the company but was unsure of how to achieve this goal. I offered to mentor them and help develop their career by providing guidance and support.

I started by meeting with my co-worker to discuss their career goals and aspirations. Together, we identified areas where they could improve and develop new skills that would make them a stronger candidate for advancement. I recommended relevant training programs and workshops that would help them acquire these skills.

I also provided ongoing feedback and encouragement to help them stay motivated and focused on their goals. I made myself available to answer any questions they had and offered advice based on my own experiences in the company.

As a result of our work together, my co-worker was able to acquire the skills and knowledge needed to advance to a higher position within the company. They were grateful for my support and credited me with helping them achieve their career goals. This experience taught me the value of mentoring and coaching in supporting the professional growth of others."

Question 92: How do you handle stress and pressure?

How do you handle stress and pressure?" is a common behavioral interview question that assesses your ability to manage challenging situations in the workplace. When answering this question, use the STAR method (Situation, Task, Action, Result) to provide a structured and detailed response:

I: Situation:

Describe a specific situation where you experienced high levels of stress or pressure in the workplace. Provide details about the context of the situation, including the nature of the stressor and the impact it had on you and your work.

II: Task:

Explain the task or goal you were working on during this stressful period. Highlight the importance of the task and the expectations or deadlines you were facing.

III: Action:

Describe the specific actions you took to manage the stress and pressure. Highlight any strategies or techniques you used to stay calm and focused, such as time management, prioritization, delegation, or seeking support from colleagues or supervisors.

IV: Result:

Explain the outcome of your efforts to handle the stress and pressure. Did you successfully complete the task or achieve your goal? How did you manage to overcome the challenges posed by the stressful situation? Reflect on what you learned from the experience and how you would approach similar situations in the future.

Example Answer:

"In my previous role, I was responsible for managing a project with a tight deadline and a high level of complexity. As the deadline approached, I started to feel overwhelmed and stressed about whether we would be able to complete the project on time.

To manage the stress and pressure, I first took a step back and assessed the situation objectively. I identified the key tasks that needed to be completed and prioritized them based on their importance and urgency. I also delegated some tasks to other team members to lighten my workload.

I then created a detailed project plan with clear milestones and deadlines to help keep myself and the team on track. I also made sure to take breaks and practice self-care to avoid burnout.

As a result of these actions, we were able to successfully complete the project on time and within budget. This experience taught me the importance of staying organized, prioritizing tasks, and seeking support from others when faced with high levels of stress and pressure."

Question 93: Describe a situation when you went above and beyond for a company?

"Describe a situation when you went above and beyond for a company" is a behavioral interview question that assesses your dedication, initiative, and willingness to go the extra mile in your work. When answering this question, use the

STAR method (Situation, Task, Action, Result) to provide a structured and detailed response:

I: Situation:

Describe the context of the situation. Provide details about the company you were working for, your role, and the specific circumstances that prompted you to go above and beyond.

II: Task:

Explain the task or goal you were working on and why it was important to the company. Highlight any challenges or obstacles you faced in achieving this task.

III: Action:

Describe the specific actions you took to go above and beyond for the company. Highlight any extra effort, creativity, or initiative you demonstrated to exceed expectations. Explain why you felt compelled to take these actions and how they contributed to the company's success.

IV: Result:

Explain the outcome of your efforts. How did your actions benefit the company? Did they lead to any tangible results or improvements? Reflect on what you learned from the experience and how it has impacted your approach to work.

Example Answer:

"In my previous role as a marketing coordinator, I was responsible for organizing a product launch event for our new line of products. As part of my role, I was tasked with creating marketing materials, coordinating with vendors, and ensuring that the event ran smoothly.

However, a week before the event, our graphic designer fell ill and was unable to complete the design work for the event banners and signage. Rather than waiting for the designer to recover, I took it upon myself to learn basic design skills and create the designs myself using online tools.

I worked late into the night for several days to complete the designs in time for the event. Despite not having any prior design experience, I was able to create professional-looking designs that were well-received by both my team and the event attendees.

As a result of my efforts, the product launch event was a great success, with many attendees commenting on the quality of the marketing materials My willingness to go above and beyond for the company not only ensured the success of the event but also demonstrated my dedication and commitment to my role."

Question 94: What's your greatest achievement?

What's your greatest achievement?" is a common interview question that allows you to showcase a significant accomplishment from your professional or personal life. When answering this question, use the STAR method (Situation, Task, Action, Result) to provide a structured and detailed response:

I: Situation:

Describe the context of your greatest achievement. Provide details about the challenge or goal you were facing and why it was significant to you or your organization.

II: Task:

Explain the specific task or goal you set out to achieve. Highlight any obstacles or challenges you encountered along the way.

III: Action:

Describe the actions you took to achieve your goal. Highlight any strategies, skills, or qualities you utilized to overcome challenges and drive success.

IV: Result:

Explain the outcome of your achievement. What were the tangible results of your efforts? How did your achievement impact you, your team, or your organization?

Example Answer:

"One of my greatest achievements was leading a cross-functional team to launch a new product that significantly increased our company's market share. In my role as project manager, I was tasked with overseeing every aspect of the product launch, from concept development to marketing and sales.

One of the biggest challenges we faced was a tight deadline for the launch, as we wanted to capitalize on a specific market opportunity. To meet this deadline, I implemented a streamlined project management process that ensured clear communication and efficient decision-making among team members.

I also worked closely with the marketing and sales teams to develop a comprehensive marketing strategy that targeted key customer segments. This included organizing a successful product launch event and coordinating with key partners and stakeholders to generate buzz around the new product.

As a result of our efforts, the product launch was a huge success, exceeding sales targets by 30% in the first quarter. The new product quickly became a bestseller in our industry and helped solidify our company's position as a market leader. This achievement not only boosted my confidence and leadership skills but also demonstrated my ability to drive results in a fast-paced and competitive environment."

Question 95: How do you stay productive under minimal supervision from a manager?

"Question 95: How do you stay productive under minimal supervision from a manager?" is a common interview question that assesses your ability to work independently and manage your time effectively. When answering this question, use the STAR method (Situation, Task, Action, Result) to provide a structured and detailed response:

I: Situation:

Describe a specific situation where you had to stay productive under minimal supervision from a manager.

Provide details about the nature of the work and the level of autonomy you had in completing it.

II: Task:

Explain the task or goal you needed to accomplish. Highlight any challenges or obstacles you faced in working without direct supervision.

III: Action:

Describe the specific actions you took to stay productive. Highlight any strategies or techniques you used to manage your time, stay organized, and prioritize tasks effectively. Explain how you stayed motivated and focused on your goals.

IV: Result:

Explain the outcome of your efforts. Did you successfully complete the task or achieve your goals? How did your ability to stay productive under minimal supervision benefit the project or organization?

Example Answer:

"In a previous role, I was responsible for managing a marketing campaign with minimal supervision from my manager. The campaign involved coordinating with multiple departments, managing a budget, and ensuring that all deliverables were completed on time.

To stay productive, I first established clear goals and milestones for the campaign. I then created a detailed project plan with timelines and deadlines for each task. This helped me stay organized and focused on what needed to be done.

I also made effective use of technology to stay connected with team members and stakeholders. I used project management software to track progress and communicate updates, and I scheduled regular check-in meetings with my manager to ensure that I was on track.

As a result of my efforts, the marketing campaign was a success, exceeding our expectations in terms of reach and engagement. My ability to stay productive under minimal supervision allowed me to effectively manage the campaign and deliver results that benefited the organization."

Question 96: Describe a time when you were flexible at work?

Describe a time when you were flexible at work?" is a behavioral interview question that assesses your ability to adapt to change and be open to new ideas or ways of working. When answering this question, use the STAR method (Situation, Task, Action, Result) to provide a structured and detailed response:

I: Situation:

Describe the context of the situation where you demonstrated flexibility at work. Provide details about the project, task, or situation you were involved in.

II: Task:

Explain the task or goal you were working on and why flexibility was required. Highlight any challenges or unexpected changes that necessitated your flexibility.

III: Action:

Describe the specific actions you took to be flexible. Highlight any changes you made to your approach, mindset, or work style to accommodate the new situation. Explain how you communicated with others and collaborated to ensure a successful outcome.

IV: Result:

Explain the outcome of your flexibility. How did your ability to be flexible benefit the project, team, or organization? What did you learn from the experience?

Example Answer:

"In a previous role, I was part of a project team working on a new product launch. As we neared the deadline, our marketing strategy was not yielding the expected results, and we needed to pivot quickly to meet our goals. This required a high level of flexibility from everyone on the team.

I suggested that we conduct a quick market survey to gather feedback from potential customers and understand their preferences better. Despite this being a departure from our original plan, the team agreed, and we quickly put together a survey and distributed it to our target audience.

Based on the feedback we received, we made several changes to our marketing strategy, including adjusting our messaging, targeting a different demographic, and using different marketing channels. This required me to be flexible in my approach and willing to adapt to new ideas and feedback.

As a result of our flexibility, we were able to improve our marketing efforts significantly and achieve our goals for the product launch. This experience taught me the importance of being open-minded and adaptable in the face of unexpected challenges."

Question 97: Describe a time when you demonstrated excellent attention to detail skills at work?

Describe a time when you demonstrated excellent attention to detail skills at work?" is a behavioral interview question that assesses your ability to focus on the specifics and maintain a high level of accuracy in your work. When answering this question, use the STAR method (Situation, Task, Action, Result) to provide a structured and detailed response:

I: Situation:

Describe the context of the situation where you demonstrated excellent attention to detail. Provide details about the project, task, or responsibility you were working on.

II: Task:

Explain the specific task or goal you were working on that required attention to detail. Highlight any challenges or complexities that made attention to detail particularly important.

III: Action:

Describe the specific actions you took to ensure accuracy and attention to detail. Highlight any strategies or techniques you used to double-check your work, review for errors, or maintain consistency.

IV: Result:

Explain the outcome of your attention to detail. How did your focus on accuracy benefit the project, team, or organization? Did it lead to any tangible results or improvements?

Example Answer:

"In my previous role as a data analyst, I was responsible for reviewing and analyzing large datasets to identify trends and patterns. During one project, I was tasked with analyzing customer feedback data to identify areas for improvement in our products.

To ensure accuracy in my analysis, I developed a detailed process for cleaning and organizing the data before conducting any analysis. This included checking for missing or duplicate data, standardizing formats, and verifying the accuracy of the data entries.

I also used data visualization tools to create charts and graphs that highlighted key findings from the data. This not only helped me identify trends more easily but also made it easier for others to understand and interpret the data.

As a result of my attention to detail, I was able to identify several key insights from the data that had not been previously recognized. These insights led to improvements in our products and services, ultimately benefiting our customers and the organization as a whole."

Question 98: What are your hobbies and interests?

What are your hobbies and interests?" is a common interview question that helps the interviewer learn more about you as a person outside of work. When answering this question, it's important to highlight hobbies and interests that demonstrate positive qualities or skills that are relevant to the job. Here's how you can approach this question:

I: Relevance:

Choose hobbies and interests that are relevant to the job or showcase valuable skills. For example, if you're applying for a role that requires teamwork, you could mention team sports or volunteer work that involves collaboration.

II: Passion:

Highlight hobbies and interests that you are genuinely passionate about. This can help demonstrate your commitment and dedication.

III: Balance:

Show that you have a balanced lifestyle by mentioning a variety of interests. This can include hobbies related to physical activity, creative pursuits, and intellectual stimulation.

IV: Skills:

Mention any skills or qualities that your hobbies have helped you develop. For example, if you enjoy photography, you could mention how it has improved your attention to detail or creativity.

V: Personalization:

Tailor your answer to the company culture. If the company values work-life balance, emphasize hobbies that demonstrate your ability to unwind and recharge outside of work.

Example Answer:

"One of my hobbies is hiking, which I find both physically rewarding and mentally refreshing. I enjoy exploring new trails and challenging myself to reach new heights. Hiking has not only improved my physical fitness but also taught me the importance of perseverance and goal-setting.

I also have a keen interest in photography, particularly nature photography. Capturing the beauty of the natural world through my lens allows me to express my creativity and attention to detail. It has also taught me patience and the ability to see things from different perspectives.

In addition, I volunteer at a local animal shelter in my free time. This allows me to give back to the community and spend time with animals, which I find incredibly rewarding. It has also honed my communication and empathy skills, as I interact with a diverse group of people and animals on a regular basis.

Overall, my hobbies and interests reflect my commitment to personal growth, creativity, and contributing to the community, which I believe align well with the values of your organization."

Question 99: What are your career goals?

What are your career goals?" is a common interview question that aims to understand your aspirations and how they align with the position and company. Here's how to approach this question:

I: Be Specific:

Outline clear and achievable career goals. Avoid vague or unrealistic statements. For example, instead of saying you want to "advance in your career," specify a particular role or skill you aim to achieve.

II: Relevance:

Tailor your goals to the job and company. Show how your goals align with the position and how achieving them would benefit the organization.

III: Short-term and Long-term Goals:

Discuss both short-term and long-term goals. Short-term goals should be achievable within a few years, while long-term goals may be more aspirational.

IV: Skills and Development:

Highlight how achieving your goals will help you develop skills and knowledge that are valuable to the role and company.

V: Company Growth:

If relevant, mention how your career goals align with the company's growth and future opportunities.

Example Answer:

"My short-term career goal is to further develop my skills and experience in [specific area related to the job], such as project management and team leadership. I aim to take on more responsibilities and lead projects to enhance my skills in these areas.

In the long term, I aspire to [specific long-term goal], such as taking on a leadership role within the organization or pursuing further education to deepen my expertise. I believe that by continuously learning and growing, I can make a significant contribution to the company and achieve personal fulfillment in my career.

I am excited about the opportunity to grow and develop within your organization, and I believe that my goals align well with the company's vision for the future. I am committed to continuous improvement and am eager to contribute to the company's success."

Question 100: That's the end of your interview. Do you have any questions for us?

That's the end of your interview. Do you have any questions for us?" This is a crucial moment in the interview where you can demonstrate your interest in the company and the role by asking thoughtful questions. Here's how to approach this question:

I: Ask About the Company:

Inquire about the company's culture, values, and future plans. This shows that you are interested in the organization as a whole, not just the job.

II: Clarify Job Expectations:

Ask about the day-to-day responsibilities of the role, the team structure, and how success is measured. This demonstrates your understanding of the position and your commitment to meeting expectations.

III: Discuss Opportunities for Growth:

Inquire about opportunities for professional development, advancement within the company, and mentorship programs. This shows that you are ambitious and committed to your career growth.

IV: Learn About the Team:

Ask about the team dynamics, the working environment, and how the team collaborates. This shows that you are interested in being a valuable team member and contributing to a positive work culture.

V: Showcase Your Knowledge:

Ask intelligent questions based on your research about the company. This demonstrates that you have done your homework and are genuinely interested in the company.

Example Questions:

(i): "Can you tell me more about the team I'll be working with and how we collaborate on projects?"

(ii): "What opportunities are there for professional development and advancement within the company?"

(iii): "How does the company support work-life balance for its employees?"

(iv): "What are some of the company's upcoming projects or initiatives that I would be involved in?"

(v): "Can you describe the company's approach to employee training and development?"

Remember, asking questions not only helps you gather important information about the job and company but also shows your enthusiasm and commitment to the role.

Chapter 5

Conclusion

A: Final Tips for Interview Success

Final tips for interview success encompass a range of strategies and techniques that can help you make a positive impression and increase your chances of landing the job. Here are some key tips:

1: Research the Company:

Before the interview, research the company's history, mission, values, products/services, and recent news or developments. This demonstrates your interest and preparedness.

2: Understand the Job Description:

Familiarize yourself with the job description and be prepared to discuss how your skills and experience align with the role.

3: Practice Common Questions:

Practice answering common interview questions, both general and job-specific, to articulate your experiences and achievements clearly.

4: Dress Appropriately:

Choose professional attire that is appropriate for the company culture and industry.

5: Arrive Early:

Plan to arrive at least 10-15 minutes early for the interview to allow time for unforeseen delays.

6: Bring Copies of Your Resume:

Bring several copies of your resume to the interview to give to the interviewer(s).

7: Listen Carefully:

Pay attention to the interviewer's questions and respond thoughtfully. Ask for clarification if you don't understand a question.

8: Use Positive Body Language:

Maintain eye contact, sit up straight, and avoid fidgeting to convey confidence and professionalism.

9: Be Concise:

Keep your answers concise and to the point, focusing on key experiences and achievements.

10: Ask Questions:

Prepare a few thoughtful questions to ask the interviewer about the company, team, or role. This demonstrates your interest and engagement.

11: Follow Up:

Send a thank-you email or note to the interviewer(s) within 24 hours of the interview to express your appreciation for the opportunity and reiterate your interest in the position.

12: Reflect on the Experience:

After the interview, take some time to reflect on what went well and what you could improve for future interviews.

By following these tips, you can present yourself effectively in interviews and increase your chances of success in landing your desired job.

B: Building Confidence for Future Interviews

Building confidence for future interviews is crucial for presenting yourself effectively and making a positive impression on potential employers. Here are some strategies to help boost your confidence:

1: Prepare Thoroughly:

Research the company, the role, and common interview questions. Practice your responses to these questions to feel more comfortable and confident.

2: Highlight Your Strengths:

Identify your key strengths and achievements and be prepared to discuss them confidently during the interview.

3: Dress for Success:

Choose professional attire that makes you feel confident and comfortable. This can help you project a positive image and feel more self-assured.

4: Practice Good Posture and Body Language:

Sit up straight, make eye contact, and use positive body language to convey confidence and professionalism.

5: Visualize Success:

Before the interview, visualize yourself succeeding and performing well. This can help boost your confidence and reduce anxiety.

6: Focus on Your Accomplishments:

Remind yourself of past successes and accomplishments to boost your confidence and remind yourself of your abilities.

7: Stay Positive:

Maintain a positive attitude and approach the interview as an opportunity to showcase your skills and experience.

8: Manage Stress:

Practice stress-reducing techniques such as deep breathing or visualization to help calm your nerves before the interview.

9: Seek Feedback:

After interviews, ask for feedback from interviewers or trusted colleagues. Use this feedback to improve and boost your confidence for future interviews.

10: Set Realistic Goals:

Set achievable goals for yourself during the interview, such as showcasing your skills or connecting with the interviewer. This can help you focus and feel more confident.

By following these strategies, you can build your confidence and improve your performance in future interviews, increasing your chances of success in landing your desired job.

C: Celebrating Your Achievements

Celebrating your achievements, whether big or small, is important for maintaining motivation, boosting self-confidence, and acknowledging your hard work. Here are some ways you can celebrate your achievements:

1: Reflect on Your Accomplishments:

Take time to reflect on what you have achieved and the progress you have made towards your goals. Acknowledge the effort and dedication it took to reach this point.

2: Share Your Success:

Share your achievements with friends, family, or colleagues who have supported you along the way. Celebrating with others can amplify your joy and sense of accomplishment.

3: Reward Yourself:

Treat yourself to something special as a reward for your hard work. This could be a small indulgence like a nice meal or a movie, or something bigger like a weekend getaway.

4: Update Your Resume or Portfolio:

Update your resume or portfolio with your latest achievements. Seeing your accomplishments in writing can reinforce your sense of pride and accomplishment.

5: Set New Goals:

Use your achievements as motivation to set new, challenging goals for yourself. This can help you maintain momentum and continue to grow personally and professionally.

6: Reflect on Lessons Learned:

Take time to reflect on the lessons you learned during the process of achieving your goal. This can help you grow and improve for future endeavors.

7: Celebrate with a Ritual:

Create a personal ritual or tradition to mark your achievements. This could be lighting a candle, writing in a journal, or simply taking a moment to savor the feeling of accomplishment.

8: Express Gratitude:

Take a moment to express gratitude for the opportunities, resources, and support that helped you achieve your goals. Gratitude can enhance your sense of well-being and happiness.

9: Share Your Story:

Share your journey and achievements with others who may benefit from your experience. Inspiring others can be a rewarding way to celebrate your achievements.

10: Celebrate the Journey, Not Just the Outcome:

Remember to celebrate the effort, growth, and learning that took place during your journey, not just the final outcome. Each step towards your goal is an achievement worth celebrating.

By celebrating your achievements, you can boost your self-confidence, maintain motivation, and cultivate a positive outlook on your future endeavors.

Read more interesting books!

www.ingramcontent.com/pod-product-compliance
Lightning Source LLC
Chambersburg PA
CBHW071206240526
45470CB00018B/1512